National and International	*Re*
July	Rapid German advance in Russia. Russians adopt "scorched earth" policy. U.S. Navy protects Allied shipping in western Atlantic from new bases in Greenland and Iceland.	M involving 170,000 troops and civil defence forces. Newmarket public houses run out of beer. Shortages of eggs and cheese.
August	Royal Navy relieves Tobruk. Roosevelt and Churchill sign the Atlantic Charter. Struggle to keep Egypt and Malta supplied. Russian resistance toughens.	Norwich "stay-at-home" Bank Holiday attracts 20,000 to Eaton Park. Farm workers awarded new 54s. per week minimum wage. New engineering block opened at Norwich City College.
September	Leningrad isolated by land, Kiev falls, Hitler orders advance on Moscow. Heavy U-boat attacks on convoys continue. Roosevelt orders attack on Axis ships in "U.S.-interested" waters.	Large-scale construction of new airfields. Coxswain Henry Blogg awarded Gold Medal of the R.N.L.I. "New invasion season" alert. Suffolk Horse Society sales at Ipswich. Mass blackberry-picking parties.
October	Battle of Atlantic at its height. R.A.F. raids Hamburg and Bremen. Moscow bombed, Soviet government moves to Kuibyshev, Leningrad besieged. German troops in Crimea. Heavy British attacks on German supply lines in Mediterranean.	Simulated German invasion of East Anglia — largest manoeuvres ever. Newmarket Bloodstock Sales. Home Secretary visits Yarmouth and Lowestoft with "keep children away" appeal. Anglo–Soviet Friendship Committees set up.
November	Severe weather and Soviet resistance halt German advance. New Allied offensive in Libya. Aircraft carrier *Ark Royal* and battleship *Barham* sunk. Malta bombed constantly.	Norfolk anti-invasion exercise. Farm workers awarded £3 per week minimum wage. Suffolk N.S.P.C.C. reports increase in cases of child neglect and assault.
December	Japanese bomb Pearl Harbour and invade Malaya, Philippines, Hong Kong and Burma. Battle cruiser *Repulse* and battleship *Prince of Wales* sunk with heavy loss of life. U.S. declares war on Axis powers. German troops in sight of Kremlin, then repulsed. Allies occupy whole of Cyrenaica, Tobruk relieved.	"Aid to Russia" weeks in all areas. Agricultural production targets set for 1942, calling for further big increases.

EAST ANGLIA 1941

Overleaf: The inhabitants of Thetford look on as an infantry tank waits outside the Bell Hotel for its turn to move forward during an exercise in April, 1941. *Imperial War Museum*

15
175

EAST ANGLIA 1941

by

R. DOUGLAS BROWN

TERENCE DALTON LIMITED
LAVENHAM . SUFFOLK
1986

Published by
TERENCE DALTON LIMITED

ISBN 0 86138 019 3

Text photoset in 10/12pt Times

Printed in Great Britain at
The Lavenham Press Limited, Lavenham, Suffolk

Contents

Publishers' Note

The publishers regret that the reproduction of certain illustrations is below the quality that they would normally demand. The *East Anglian Daily Times* and the *Eastern Daily Press*, who kindly permitted us the use of their files, were unfortunately unable to provide original photographs and, consequently, the pictures shown are reproductions from the printed newspapers. The same applies to those photographs acknowledged to the *Cambridge Evening News* that were so kindly provided by the Cambridge Collection of the Cambridgeshire Libraries. Where applicable, it was considered preferable to show illustrations, even if below our usual standard, rather than no pictures at all. This volume is the third of a series which will fully document the events in East Anglia, year by year, and we would welcome any photographs that apply to 1942 or subsequent years. These would be forwarded to the author for his use and, of course, returned in due course.

Index of Illustrations

Introduction and Acknowledgements

THIS is the third volume of a series which, when completed, will be a unique record of the wartime years 1939–45 in one particular region of Britain. No similar publication has been attempted for any other region, and this is likely to prove the most detailed chronological account of the circumstances of the everyday life of the civilian population during those testing years.

The year reviewed in this volume lacked the dramatic excitements of 1940, when East Anglia was in the front line during the Battle of Britain; it lacked, too, the physical and cultural upheavals of 1942, when dozens of new air bases were constructed in the region and many thousands of Americans crossed the Atlantic to man them. In one sense, 1941 was a year when "nothing much happened". The German forces had won the early battles of the war and the Allies were not yet ready to fight the later, decisive campaigns. It was a time of waiting, and of preparation.

But daily life as it was experienced then, with all the inconveniences of the blackout, the ever-worsening food shortages, the calling to arms, to civil defence and to the munitions factories of ever-increasing numbers of men and women, was as integral a part of the experience of war as were the exploits of the men in the tanks and the planes and the battleships. It is of the routines of home life during the darkest hours of wartime that this book tells: the special day trips to neighbouring towns when it was rumoured that one might buy oranges or chocolates there; the controversy about the employment of mothers in factories, and the consternation of young girls because their call-up would reveal their ages; the astonishing efforts made to collect salvage and to stimulate savings; the labours of elderly men on their allotments and of women in their kitchens. It is in the minutiae of that existence that one best captures the flavour of the period.

It had not been my original intention to compile this volume, but circumstances prevented the intended author from completing his task. I have, therefore, resumed the narrative which I began in *East Anglia 1939* and *East Anglia 1940*, and which I shall hope to complete in later volumes. I have worked, however, with the results of research done by other hands, and I wish to record my indebtedness to them. I have supplemented their information in various ways, and I have set the regional picture in the frame of the national and international situation at the time. In doing this, I have rested heavily on the various official histories of the war and on

A scene that was typical of 1941: women "bombed out" of their homes in Vauxhall Street, Norwich, gather outside their wrecked houses to talk things over. *George Swain*

The Grand Alliance, the third volume of Sir Winston Churchill's classic history of the war. The theme which I have developed, which I believe to be the essential characteristic of 1941, is that of a people battered to their knees and slowly and painfully rising again, regaining their breath, winning allies, and preparing to hit back.

A great deal of the information in this book had been collected from the regional newspapers, and thanks are expressed to their publishers and editors. Because of the restrictions on photography during the war years, most of the photographs have come from this same source, and, because the negatives and original prints have not been preserved, it has been necessary to re-photograph them, a process which regrettably involves some loss of definition. Extracts have been printed from diaries kept during 1941 by five men and women living in different parts of the region, and I have to express thanks to the custodians of the Mass Observation Archive at Sussex University, in which these diaries are preserved. Because the diarists were promised confidentiality, their identities are concealed by pseudonyms. Extracts have also been used from reports prepared during 1941 by Mass Observation representatives who made special visits to the region to gather material.

R. DOUGLAS BROWN

Stoke-by-Clare, Suffolk.
April, 1986.

CHAPTER ONE

Alone, Against All Odds

NEVER in history was Britain in more dire straits or confronted with more bleak a prospect than in the first few days of January, 1941. The indomitable national leader, Winston Churchill, afterwards admitted that there was no other time during the war of 1939-45 when he and his colleagues felt under such stress, as the problems piled up before them.[1] All who lived through those days would later be able to look back over the seasons of their lives and declare that this was "the very dead of winter".

Britain, after sixteen months at war with Germany, stood alone. On the European mainland, every coastline was manned by hostile forces. Norway, Denmark, the Netherlands, Belgium and France had all been overcome and occupied. The Luftwaffe now had bases within a few hundred miles of the great industrial and commercial centres of this country; its bombers could easily attack not only targets in the United Kingdom but also convoys of shipping far out in the Atlantic bringing supplies upon which the very survival of the British people depended. The German navy, seeking to fasten down a complete blockade, had the use of virtually every port from the northernmost tip of Norway to the Bay of Biscay.

British forces had taken a beating. Though the evacuation of 400,000 Allied troops from Dunkirk in the early summer of 1940 had been presented as a triumph, it was a triumph of improvisation; the harsh reality was that the B.E.F. had been defeated and driven from the soil of Europe and practically the whole of their heavy equipment and vast quantities of stores had been left behind. The Battle of Britain, which followed in August and September, was indeed a British triumph, for it destroyed Hitler's hopes of invading Britain. But in the course of that titanic struggle the Royal Air Force lost nearly 1,000 aircraft and many brave pilots. At sea, the situation was equally desperate. The Royal Navy had insufficient vessels to protect the convoys, and shipping losses had been mounting month by month.

This was not, of course, the picture that was presented to the British people through the official channels of information. But enough was known — enough evidence was daily before their eyes — for them to have a general apprehension of the grim realities. And there was no way the facts could be concealed when, within sixty hours of the end of the year, German incendiary bombs started 1,500 fires in the City of London and many famous buildings were destroyed.

Essex farmers regularly gave their "surplus" vegetables to the crews of minesweeping trawlers based at Parkeston Quay, according to the wartime caption of this photograph showing the ships' cooks receiving their allocation. *Imperial War Museum*

It was obvious, too, that Britain was ill equipped to defend itself against such attacks. The public did not actually *know* that the anti-aircraft batteries were inadequately equipped, with insufficient guns, virtually no effective assistance from radar devices and only a rudimentary control system on the ground; or that the R.A.F. was still desperately trying to train more pilots for night operations, but it could make its own wise decisions. During air raids people crouched in their shelters, under the stairs or beneath their tables, and got what comfort they could from the noise of the barrage put up by the A.A. batteries; but they realised all too clearly that the bombers kept coming, wave after wave.

The reality of a country under siege could be understood quite as well by those who lived in remote rural areas of East Anglia as by those in the great cities, though the evidence was of a different kind. Almost everywhere property had been commandeered in which to billet troops. New service facilities, airfields, hutted camps, defence barriers, were being built all over the region. At Bury St Edmunds, for example, the established depot of the Suffolk Regiment at Gibraltar Barracks could not cope with the flow of recruits and a new hutted camp, known as "West Lines", was being built on the Newmarket Road, with modern cook-houses and dining halls, company offices and lecture halls.[(2)] Much of the building work was done by private contractors, sometimes employing refugees who had escaped to Britain before the advance of the Nazis.

As 1941 began, several of the East Anglian battalions were being switched from the construction of coastal defences to basic training. The 4th and 5th battalions of the Suffolks were in the vanguard; they were based near St Neots and in Cambridge respectively and they did their best to train while their equipment and transport was trickling through to them and construction went on all around them. Conditions were difficult. An officer with a literary flair, writing about conditions near Cambridge at the time, gave this vivid account:

> We have now got on much friendlier terms with the mud into which, however, half the by-products of an asbestos factory and a platoon truck were sunk without any visible trace whatever . . . Life goes on. The skeletons of elegant, graceful structures appear outside the Company office, to the husky incantation of wild gypsy songs from central Europe; even when the cement-mixer is going, you can smell Spring as it comes to the upper reaches of the Moldau.[(3)]

Most of the East Anglian battalions became part of the 18th Division, which, as soon as it got its hands on sufficient equipment and transport, was ordered to mobilise to proceed overseas. In fact in January, 1941, it moved to Scotland, continued its training there, and mobilised up to full strength. Life was not much easier there; the weather was terrible, with field exercises taking place in blizzards and snow lying nine inches deep at some of the camps. But there were some compensations; the people of Dumfries, Galashiels and Hawick were hospitable, there were canteens, dances and picture houses, and sirens were only sounded for practice purposes. The Free Norwegian Army was also stationed in Dumfries, and its soldiers seemed to have more money to spend than the East Anglian lads, and that could be frustrating during off-duty hours.

Several new battalions had been formed in East Anglia with men newly recruited in the call-ups of 1939 and 1940. The 6th battalion of the Suffolk Regiment was formed in August, 1939, with its headquarters at the Drill Hall in Portman Road at Ipswich. Soon afterwards three companies recruited from Bury St Edmunds, Saxmundham and Cambridge were formed into the 2/6th, with headquarters at Bury, and in January, 1941, the 2/6th became the 9th battalion, Suffolk Regiment, the 7th and 8th battalions having been formed in May, 1940. The 7th moved off almost immediately to Dorset, where it constructed and then manned beach defences around Studland Bay, between Bournemouth and Swanage. The 8th, as 1941 began, had just completed similar duties, erecting steel scaffolding over the beaches at Walton and Frinton. This was sometimes frustrating. Their commanding officer later admitted that:

> a feature of the construction of these defences was their frequent alteration. All senior officers, from the Army Commander and Corps Commander downwards, had their views on the siting of section posts, and after their frequent visits corresponding adjustments usually had to be made.(3)

While performing home defence duties these battalions were given some basic training, but there were so few weapons available, and other equipment and

Members of the Suffolk Regiment are inspected by the Corps commander after taking part in an exercise which has obviously destroyed the polish on their boots. *East Anglian Daily Times*

transport was so scarce, that it was usually for only a few hours each week. The 7th battalion, in fact, was playfully designated "the string and cardboard Suffolks", because the men went around with their civilian gasmasks in their original cardboard boxes.

Those who lived near the coast in East Anglia were constantly reminded of one area of the war in which there was *too much* action. The trawlers and drifters of Great Yarmouth and Lowestoft sailed each day to sweep the sea lanes where the Germans were constantly and successfully laying minefields — so successfully that for a while the East Coast convoys had to be restricted. Luftwaffe fighters and light bombers came regularly over the North Sea and dive-bombed and machine-gunned

Men of the Suffolk Regiment, accompanied by their Bren gun carriers, taking part in an exercise. The corporal carries a Thompson sub-machine gun, one of the weapons received from America during the early war years.
East Anglian Daily Times

any vessel they sighted. German E-boats prowled constantly, sometimes hiding in the shadow of buoys quite close to the coast and attacking convoys suddenly. But the minefields were the principal danger. As 1941 began, the Royal Naval Patrol Service had already lost more than 140 vessels, and the situation was getting worse; two or three vessels were lost or severely damaged every week. In January, for example, the Trinity House tender *Strathearn* struck a mine off Clacton and sank, and fifteen of the crew, including the master, Captain R.S. Raven, were killed.[4]

R.A.F. Hurricanes flying from Martlesham Heath and Coltishall patrolled the convoy lanes and did their best to keep the Luftwaffe at bay. Until mid-March No 242 Squadron at Martlesham was led by the legless Douglas Bader.

This was the sea-war at close quarters, but it was obvious that more serious dangers threatened in the Atlantic. A large part of the food supplies essential to survival and a great deal of war equipment urgently required by the forces was coming from Canada and the United States. The convoys were regularly attacked. In the early months of 1941 the shipyards were becoming clogged with more vessels awaiting repair than they could handle, and the Germans had managed to mine the approaches to all the principal ports.[5]

The paddle minesweeper *Lorna Doone,* in peacetime operating as a pleasure steamer in the Southampton and Isle of Wight area, after she had beaten off an attack by three German bombers. Although already an old vessel, having been built in 1891, she was converted later into an auxiliary anti-aircraft vessel to give protection to coastal convoys. The censor has erased the pendant number from her bows.
East Anglian Daily Times

Life was bleak for the civilian population. Those housewives who had prudently stockpiled their larders in the early months of the war had long since exhausted their reserves. Jenny Carr, one of two sisters living with their mother in Snettisham, Norfolk, noted in her diary in mid-January:

> Mother has, for the first time, begun to have tea without sugar. Until now, she has insisted on using it, as our hoard grew less.

Now rationing was getting tougher every week. On 3rd January the *Cambridge Daily News* reported that all kinds of liver, kidney, heart and sweetbreads would henceforth be rationed, as well as the head, cheek, tongue and tail of oxen. On 10th January it was announced that treacle and syrup was to be rationed. The following day the allocation of meat to butchers was cut to half of the previous supply, and the butchers of Bury St Edmunds and district decided they might as well close their shops on three days each week. The weekly ration per person now became twelve to eighteen-pence worth, according to the type of meat purchased.

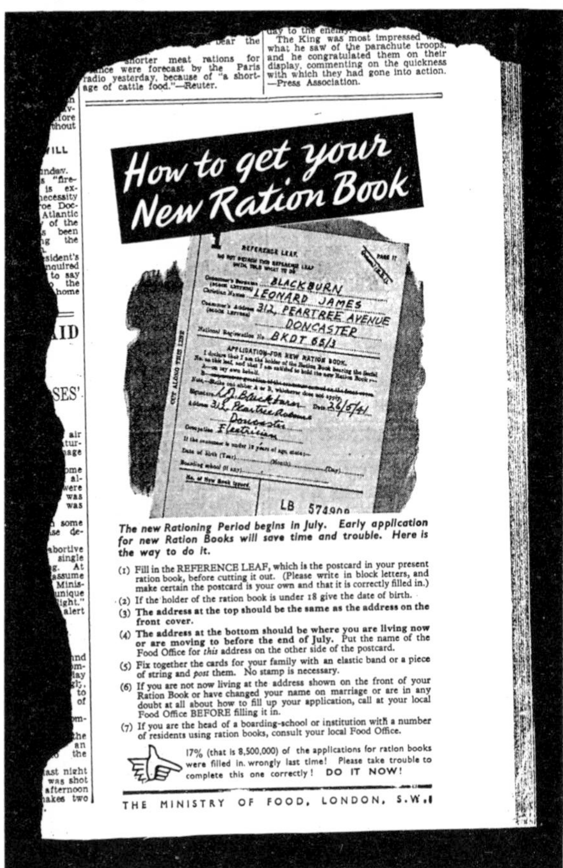

An advertisement inserted in local newspapers by the Ministry of Food telling people how to apply for their new ration books.
East Anglian Daily Times

Jenny Carr's family kept a garage and a small village shop, and at the end of the month she noted:

> All the other shops in the village have been sold out of sweets and chocolates for several weeks. We had a big stock, and now it is down to about one shilling's worth. Several people have bought some for hoarding, coming every day, buying in instalments. The wholesale dealers don't seem to have had any sweets or chocolates for months now.

Even for the things that were not rationed, shopping had become a strange and new experience. For example, from January, 1941, one could buy only "standard emergency furniture", which was manufactured to an austere utility formula.

The strict imposition of a blackout after dark was another burden to be borne. The number of road accidents had increased significantly, despite the fact there were fewer vehicles on the roads because of petrol rationing. Many cyclists were fined for riding without lights, the usual excuse being that they had been unable to obtain batteries. Some were prosecuted for flashing lights unnecessarily, while a girl in the Women's Land Army in Cambridgeshire was fined because she *did not* flash a torch in front of a herd of cows she was leading, with the result that a motorist ran into them.

Travel was difficult. There were fewer private cars on the roads; the trains were often seriously delayed, unheated, and crowded with Servicemen. Most people used the buses, but there were difficulties with them. On 24th January the Eastern Counties Omnibus Company advised the public not to travel during the rush hours, when the buses were packed with workers. Petrol rationing applied as much to public service vehicles as to private cars, the company said, added to which the military had taken over many of their buses at almost a moment's notice.

Elsewhere in the region, Cecil Sparks, who was a special constable, noted in his diary:

> On one local route a single-decker bus is being run which has been converted to carry 61 passengers, instead of 43 . . . I hear that a front tyre burst the other day. Fortunately, the bus was just pulling up when it happened. Travelling at 30 m.p.h., this might have had serious consequences. Let's hope the matter is being investigated. . .

Over this sombre scene Nature perversely cast its own bleak blanket of ice and snow. Parts of East Anglia were under drifts four and five feet deep during January. Especially around Great Yarmouth and Lowestoft, bus services were interrupted and cars were abandoned in drifts on some main roads. The weather experts declared that it was not as cold as it had been during the January of 1940, but that was no solace — it was indeed the second coldest January since the beginning of the century. And any optimism about an early end to the war, which might have sustained the public a year earlier, had been banished.

It was against this bleak background that General Jan Smuts, the South African leader, greeted the New Year with a warning that an invasion of the United Kingdom might occur soon.

The people met the grim realities of the situation head-on. They showed resignation, but also fortitude and a determination to battle on until the job to which they had set their hands had been completed. But they also seemed determined to maintain the normal routines of their ordinary lives as far as possible.

Glancing through the pages of the *Cambridge Daily News* during January they were offered a choice between a pantomime at the Arts Theatre, films showing at eight different cinemas, a whole range of concerts, plays and exhibitions, and football matches at the weekends. On New Year's Eve more than 500 dancers made a record crowd at Cambridge Guildhall, there were 600 others at the Dorothy Cafe (where "dancing ended early in the morning with hearty

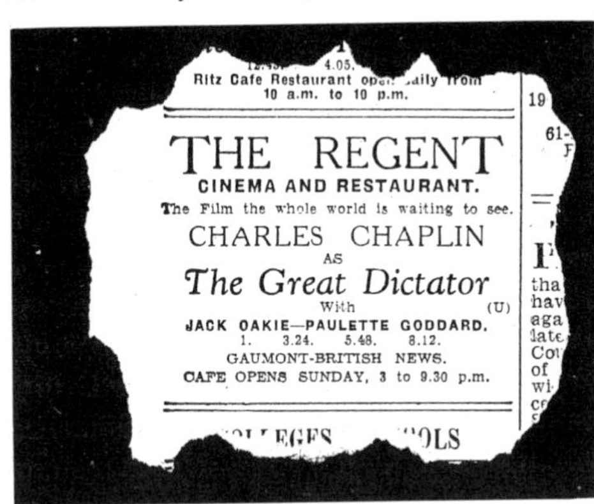

Left: An advertisement from the *East Anglian Daily Times* for the showing of a famous Charlie Chaplin film at an Ipswich cinema.

Opposite: British Power Boat Company 60-foot motor torpedo boats of the 1st M.T.B. Flotilla at Parkeston Quay. This flotilla was the first to be based at H.M.S. *Beehive*, the Coastal Forces base at Felixstowe Dock. The destroyer lying at a buoy in the Stour, H.M.S. *Wivern*, has a false bow wave painted on her bows to deceive an enemy about her speed. *Imperial War Museum*

cheers"), and 500 more at the Rex Ballroom, which advertised dances every evening.

Some events exhibited a fine indifference to the harsh environment. The Norfolk and Norwich branch of the English Folk Dance and Song Society presented a programme of English folk music in the St Giles' Parish Hall in Norwich to raise money for the rebuilding of the national headquarters of the society, Cecil Sharp House. Inevitably, much of the entertainment carried overtones of war. The New Year Carnival Dance at Downham Market was organised by the Troops' Welfare Committee. The films shown at the cinemas were nearly all of one *genre*: at the Electric Theatre in Norwich, for example, from 1st January, Clive Brook in *Convoy* — "a thrilling naval drama" — and a second film called *Hitler, Beast of Berlin*. But the most remarkable surrender to the spirit of the time was at Colchester, where it was decreed that no "Axis music" — by which was meant anything by a German or Italian composer — should be played at a concert at the Technical College in aid of the Red Cross!

So how, in so fraught a situation, could the opinion-formers — the statesmen and politicians and editorial writers — give an effective lead to the public? They found a triple theme. Firstly, the fight would be long and arduous. The *Eastern Daily Press*, surveying the year ahead, grimly observed: "While our hopes look beyond it, we are very conscious that we have to go through it". Secondly, though Britain stood alone, it had a powerful friend. In the words of the *Bury Free Press* leader-writer, "The United States would never acquiesce in a peace dictated by aggressors, sponsored by appeasers". And, thirdly, there was a better society to be achieved when the war was eventually over. The *Bury Free Press* was particularly firm about this: "We must seek social justice and industrial peace," its leader-writer argued. There would have to be a wages policy, so that no family need be undernourished; a new spirit was already moving among the people.

The key to the immediate future did, in fact, rest in the hands of the United States. Prime Minister Winston Churchill was quite convinced of that. From the day he had become the war leader, Churchill had kept in almost daily contact with President Franklin D. Roosevelt and now, at the turn of the year, he was pleading most urgently with him. After Dunkirk vast supplies of American equipment crossed the Atlantic, but it all had to be paid for; Churchill knew (though few others were told) that by the beginning of 1941 Britain had spent all its available gold and foreign assets. On 10th January Roosevelt's personal envoy, Mr Harry Hopkins, carried to 10 Downing Street the terse message: "The President is determined that we shall win the war together".(6)

The *Bury Free Press* – and the other East Anglian papers which spoke of American goodwill as the guarantee of Britain's future — knew exactly what they were talking about. The "guidance" from the Ministry of Information was based upon the highest authority.

CHAPTER TWO

Taking Punishment

BEFORE things could begin to get better, they were going to get worse. After the Battle of Britain in 1940 and German recognition that they could not attempt invasion of the United Kingdom in that year, it became a war of attrition. The Luftwaffe Command transferred about a hundred additional aircraft from German bases to reinforce the bomber units which had taken part in the all-out air assault on Britain in the previous summer.

Winston Churchill, in a speech on 17th January, warned: "Before us lie many months of having to endure a bombardment of our cities and industrial areas, without the power to make equal reply."

Bombing was already familiar to the public by then. A programme of night raids on built-up areas had begun in September, 1940, and it continued until May, 1941, by which time there had been seventy-one major raids in London and fifty-six on other large urban centres. The bombs became more destructive as time passed. During 1940 only one per cent of them had exceeded 250 kilograms; in 1941 this proportion increased to five per cent, and some weighed 1,000 and 2,500 kilograms.[(1)] There was destruction of property on a massive scale, and thousands of people died, but factories and transport kept going and production and distribution were not halted.

The best that the Royal Air Force could manage by way of response was a series of raids on German ports and hit-and-run attacks on factories in German-occupied France and Belgium. Many of these raids were mounted from bases in East Anglia, and local folk grew accustomed to the noise of planes taking off and returning.

Nowhere in East Anglia suffered from these raids on anything like the scale of London, Liverpool, Coventry and Plymouth, yet neither did the region escape the attention of the raiders. During 1940 Italian as well as German bombers had attacked East Coast towns, but ineffectively. Now they dropped out of the picture completely; the last time Italian warplanes were seen in East Anglia was on 2nd January, when five of them appeared over Ipswich. No damage was reported. But the Luftwaffe gave no respite, and there were few places in the Eastern Counties, urban or rural, where their bombers did not appear, and most towns suffered serious damage during the first half of the year.

The R.A.F. stations in the Eastern Counties were regularly attacked. Great Yarmouth, Lowestoft and other coastal towns attracted almost continuous attention and suffered most grievously, and Norwich and Ipswich also took regular punishment.

Bombing of Norwich had begun back in June, 1940. By the time the new year opened, several of the principal industrial concerns in the city had organised a joint system of "spotting" enemy planes as part of their air raid precautions. The observation post was a steel pylon tower with a cabin and a surrounding gallery at the top, erected in the grounds of 15 Bracondale in Norwich. The firms involved in the scheme were Boulton and Paul Ltd., Laurence, Scott and Electromotors Ltd., R.J. Read Ltd., Reckitt and Colman Ltd., and the London and North Eastern Railway Company. The man who took charge of the operation was Second Officer E.S. West of the Carrow Works Fire Brigade and Police. "The early records of 1941 show that visits by enemy aircraft were frequent, and that life on the gallery of the Observation Post was a chilly business," he recalled later.(2)

There was a limited raid on the city on 5th January, but little damage was caused and there were no casualties. A month later, on 4th February, on a very dark night, several planes arrived over the Norwich area at about 9 p.m. and dropped bombs a little to the north of the city. One of them scored a direct hit on the joinery shop at Boulton and Paul's with a high explosive bomb. Three houses were also wrecked that night, two people being killed and five injured. One of those who died was at work in the Thorpe Station goods yard.

An observation post which was erected in the grounds of 15 Bracondale in Norwich as part of an air raid warning system operated jointly by a number of industrial firms in the city. *Colman Foods*

In a raid on 18th February seven people were killed when a heavy explosive bomb demolished the Vauxhall Tavern, two houses in Vauxhall street and one in Walpole Street. The size of the craters and the area of devastation was greater than anything seen in the city after earlier raids. About fifty houses were sufficiently damaged that night to make 150 people homeless. Eleven houses on one side of Vauxhall Street and four on the other side were completely demolished. Rescue workers, wardens and neighbours who had survived the night dug for hours in the rubble. Mobile canteens arrived to offer them food and hot drinks.

On 27th February a lone Heinkel He. 111 bombed and machine-gunned the ironworks of Barnards Ltd., who advertised themselves as "Gate and Railing Makers to H.M. The King", from about 200 feet. The bombs hit unused buildings and there was no interruption to production, but several employees came under machine-gun fire and had narrow escapes from death. There were further raids during the nights of 14th-15th and 30th-31st March, but in these the damage was limited and no-one was killed, although incendiary bombs scattered in the Tombland area started some small fires.

The public took the raids calmly. On 19th February Miss Jenny Carr made a day trip from Snettisham to Norwich and returned home to record in her diary:

> Alert sounded during lunch and the All Clear one hour later. No-one appeared to take the slightest notice, except that a roof spotter appeared on the roof across the road from the restaurant window. Norwich seemed as busy as in pre-war days, and the shops were stocked much better than those in Lynn.

On 10th February, although no raid developed, Norwich had its longest Alert; the sirens wailed to give warning of danger at 6.48 p.m., and the All Clear was not

Left: The morning after a heavy bomb had demolished houses in Vauxhall Street, Norwich, workmen begin to seal off gas and water mains; residents have already salvaged what belongings they can from the wrecked houses. *George Swain*

Right: Policemen keep watch as Corporation officials and workmen assess the damage in Vauxhall Street. *George Swain*

sounded until 6.59 the following morning. During the month of March there were 145 warnings and the city stood at Alert for a total of 177 hours — almost for one hour in every four. This situation caused such disorganisation that during March a new system of "Crash" or "air raid imminent" warnings was instituted, the siren being treated simply as an "alert". People stayed at their jobs until the observers close at hand signalled that the enemy planes were almost overhead by sounding a series of short blasts on the city's factory hooters.

Even so a single plane could sometimes create havoc. On 2nd April, in daylight, a Dornier Do.215 arrived under cover of low cloud and went into a shallow dive over the city. Dropping from 1,500 to 900 feet and emerging from the cloud, the German took aim and placed two heavy H.E. bombs right on target, the first on the Boulton and Paul factory — more or less where bombs had fallen two months before — and the second on the goods yard at Thorpe Station, where one person was killed.

In the early hours of 8th April more incendiaries rained down on the city. Some fell on the Riverside Works of Boulton and Paul and were dealt with by workers there before they did any damage. There was a more serious attack on 29th April, just as many people were going to bed. Boulton and Paul firefighters again went into action and prevented any serious damage, but elsewhere things did not go as well. A string of H.E. bombs hit Reckitt and Colman's Carrow Works in King Street; the oatmeal mill and mustard department were set alight, and the flames spread to the wheat and flour mills. It took five hours for the Carrow Works Fire Brigade, operating alongside the Norwich City Brigade and an Auxiliary Fire Service unit, to bring the blaze under control. The mills were gutted. One man was killed at Carrow, and elsewhere an elderly woman died. High explosive bombs fell in several parts of the city. In one incident, on Carrow Hill, a gas main was fractured and caught fire, and there was a red glow over the whole area which lit up the spire of the cathedral.

By May the periods of Alert were greatly reduced, but the raids did not stop altogether. The industrial establishments escaped, but many private homes were destroyed; on successive nights, 6th and 7th May, eight people were killed and several injured. Unthank Road and Bury Street suffered in the first raid, Earlham

Women search the ruins of their houses in Vauxhall Street, Norwich, salvaging as many of their treasured possessions as they can.
George Swain

(where 150 people were made homeless) in the second. Five members of a family of eight were killed in one house; a fragment of shrapnel flew through the front door of the house next door and landed on a pram with a ten-month-old baby in it, but the child was unhurt because a fireguard had been placed over the pram as protection. There were many tales of such providential escapes from death and injury.

Some of the raids on Norwich appear to have been sideshows to major assaults on the East Coast ports. The officer in charge of the observation post serving the city's factories explained: "An analysis of the tracks of enemy planes over Norfolk shows that their paths converged over the Norwich area, and frequently when a raid was concentrated on a coastal district, one or more planes would pay a short visit to this area."[3]

Great Yarmouth and Lowestoft were very much in the front line during this phase. Enemy planes flew in almost daily, bombing and machine-gunning. Sixty per cent of the population of this coastal belt had been evacuated in 1940, otherwise the casualties would certainly have been appalling. But the ordeal was terrible, nonetheless, as an account of the events of two nights during April will make clear. More property was destroyed in Great Yarmouth during the night of 7th-8th April than in any other wartime raid on East Anglia.

The first of the attacking planes appeared overhead just after midnight and scattered incendiary bombs on open ground to the west of the town, doubtless intended to serve as markers for the waves of bombers that followed. About half an hour later two mines drifted down on parachutes. They fell among houses in the Collingwood Road area in the northern part of the town, from which most of the residents had been evacuated in 1940, so that only two people were killed and seven injured. As the police and civil defence forces went into action, more planes arrived overhead and showered a very large number of explosive incendiary bombs over much of the town; they fell over an area which extended from the market place southwards, across the Rows area and into Gorleston, starting many serious fires. Soon, virtually every human being in the areas affected was committed to firefighting, the regular fire brigade and the recently formed Auxiliary Fire Service units being joined by policemen, special constables, air raid wardens, street firefighting parties and members of the general public. At the Fire Control Room and Report Centre, Chief Constable C.G. Box (who was also the controller of the civil defence forces) realised that the scale of the problem was greater than could be handled by the forces at his command.[4] The fires were so widespread and numerous that they could not be reached before they had flared to spectacular proportions. And, all the time, more German planes were coming in from the North Sea and scattering more incendiary bombs. Just after 2 a.m. the Chief Constable called for assistance from Lowestoft and Beccles, and about fifty minutes later he asked the Regional Controller's office at Cambridge to organise additional help. Fire brigades and civil defence forces were then despatched post-haste from Norwich and Cromer.

The ordeal became more intense hour by hour as the night passed. Two large H.E. bombs fell on Southtown Road and made craters so large that vehicles could no longer pass between Great Yarmouth and Gorleston. They also fractured some water mains, causing a drop in pressure in Yarmouth, which hindered the firefighters further. A few minutes after 5 a.m. two more mines drifted down on parachutes and their explosion caused havoc in the southern part of the town. One exploded at the junction of Blackfriars Road and Queens Road, where a Special Constabulary sub-station received the full force of the blast and five special constables were killed; the other fell at the south end of Middlegate Street, in the

Rows area. Here the devastation was immense; among the buildings which were gutted or seriously damaged were the Seamen's Mission, the old Tolhouse museum and the adjoining public library, the education offices, the Science School, and very many commercial premises, including Marks and Spencers, Boots the Chemists, Hill's Restaurant, Rose's Fashions and Johnson's clothing factory. As the Chief Constable weighed the reports of the further damage, he called to Norwich for more assistance, and three rescue parties were quickly on their way.

By the time that night had ended (it was later estimated), the Luftwaffe had dropped 4,000 incendiary bombs on Great Yarmouth and Gorleston, and had started sixty-five major blazes and nearly two hundred other fires. Chief Constable Box afterwards wrote:

> I shall never forget the appalling sight that Yarmouth presented that night. With the additional fires that continually broke out, it seemed that nothing could prevent the destruction of the centre of the town and South Quay. But when day broke, owing to the untiring efforts of all concerned, all fires were under control and the situation, although bad, was saved from becoming worse.

Seventeen people died and sixty-eight were injured during the night, but, amazingly, no casualties arose from the incendiary bombs and the fires which they caused.

The civil defence and other services were given no respite for, after working strenuously throughout the following day to clear the streets and get their own organisations back into good shape, they found the Luftwaffe overhead again within hours. At 9.30 p.m. on the 8th four H.E. bombs were dropped at the south end of the borough, and about an hour and a half later a large number of incendiaries fell on to premises on both sides of the River Yare. In one big blaze,

This massive bomb, apparently aimed by a Heinkel He. 111 at Ipswich gasworks, failed to explode when it fell into soft ground in Holywells Park, Ipswich. It is seen after being dug out by a Royal Engineers bomb disposal team. *Ian Scrivener*

Firefighters at work in the main shopping street of Yarmouth during the air raid on the night of 7th–8th April. The fires gained such a hold that assistance had to be brought in from other parts of Norfolk and North Suffolk. *Imperial War Museum*

the Salt Union premises were completely gutted, but elsewhere the firefighters, despite their weariness, were able to extinguish the fires before much damage was done.

Early in June there were two more heavy raids on Great Yarmouth. On the night of 6th-7th twelve people were killed and four seriously injured, and two nights later two more were killed and 120 houses and shops and a church were demolished. Serious damage was caused to a thousand other houses, to a fire station, a first-aid post, to the railway, and to some utility services.

Lowestoft, too, went through grim times. In one February raid the St Peter's Street area was badly damaged, and in a raid on 6th March the Lowestoft Free Library was completely demolished. On 9th-10th April, in the worst raid of the year, twenty-two people were killed and thirty-nine injured, and Austin and Wales'

The medieval church at Pakefield which was largely destroyed by fire after incendiary bombs had been dropped during an air raid in May. *Eastern Daily Press*

wholesale grocery warehouse was destroyed. On 5th May Woolworth's and Timpson's boot and shoe shop were almost levelled. In May, too, the parish church at Pakefield was extensively damaged.

It was a recognition of the special ordeal of the people of Great Yarmouth and Lowestoft that on 25th April the Duke of Kent visited bombed areas in the two towns. He talked not only to the civic authorities and the fire service, civil defence and police, but also to many individuals who had suffered loss. He met one eighty-one-year-old fisherman who was standing staring at the ruins of the home in which, he said, he had lived for fifty-nine years.

Most towns in the region received some attention. At King's Lynn, for example, the dock area was bombed on 13th March and one side of the coal hoist on the Bentinck Dock was fractured. On 6th May in the same town two council houses on Baggs Road were demolished; although the residents were buried under the rubble when the roof collapsed on top of them, they escaped without serious injury. The Gaywood Estate was being built at the time and Queen Mary Road had been camouflaged with colour-wash or paint; local people surmised that the German pilot had mistaken this road for an airfield runway.

Lynn suffered a much more serious raid on Monday, 12th June, when The

Friars was bombed. Boal Street was completely destroyed and parts of Whitefriars Terrace and Bridge Street damaged, the old *Ship Inn* on the corner being completely wrecked. The manager and his wife had lucky escapes; both were blown the whole length of the passage-way. A description of that episode was recorded by A.R.P. warden B.R. Hart:

> The smell was awful as the sewers were broken. We searched for two litle boys, but found them both in bed, dead. The Army set up lights and when enemy aircraft were reported in the vicinity these were switched off. During one of these breaks we heard a faint scream, and as soon as the lights came on again we worked hard to uncover a complete wood floor. We broke a hole into it and shone a torch, calling out if anybody could see the light. A voice replied "Yes, please hurry up and get me out, I'd like a cup of tea." When we got to the voice, it was a young girl. She wasn't badly hurt. We next searched for another woman, but she was dead when we got to her. As it was getting near 7 a.m. and time for me to go to work, I knocked off. On the way home, Mr Preston Rush, of the Crossways, asked me in for a cup of hot drink and rum. It was very welcome.(5)

Sixteen people from Boal Street and Whitefriars Terrace died in this raid. Mr Albert E. Stringer, of 11 Whitefriars Terrace, was working on night shift when the bombs fell and found when he arrived home at the end of the shift that his house had received a direct hit. His wife was pinned by the legs under the debris, but was singing when the rescuers reached her; she did not know that her two children had been killed. Similarly, eighteen-year-old George Thurlow was pulled from the wreckage of 1 Boal Street, only slightly injured and shocked, but had then to be told that his father had been killed.

While this rescue work was going on, more bombs were dropped on South Lynn. One fell on allotments and one near a railway bridge, leaving craters twenty feet across, and the Greenland Fishery Museum was badly damaged and many of its exhibits lost.

A raid on the Walton district of Felixstowe on 12th May left 280 premises damaged. Eight houses were completely destroyed and many others damaged in King Street and Maidstone Road by the eight bombs dropped, and among four people killed was a two-day-old baby. Ten people were seriously injured, and seven others slightly hurt.

At the time, of course, the newspapers were not allowed to publish any geographical detail about these raids, so that much of the information was spread by word of mouth and naturally became distorted in the process. Clues were sometimes provided as, for example, by the *Cambridge Daily News* when on 16th January it reported that "incendiary bombs were dropped on an East Anglian town" and then added that the place had "a famous public school dating back to about 1600", a hospital and a famous church. This was intended to give local residents the facts without giving much away to the enemy.

Photographs could be published, provided they did not enable the location to be established, and editors often considered these the most satisfactory way of presenting an overall impression of the war on the home front, supplemented by the generalised descriptive matter that could be printed. Thus, during the course of January, Cambridge readers were given pictures of two sets of air raid damage, and were told that on the 4th a Dornier bomber had been chased away by British fighters, watched by people in an unidentified town; on the 7th shoppers had taken cover when an enemy raider appeared over an East Anglian town; on the 8th there had been a raider "near an East Anglian town"; and on the 16th the incendiaries had fallen on the town with the public school, the hospital and the famous church; and on the 31st a Congregational church and some houses had been damaged in a daytime raid on another town.

Alternatively, more specific detail was sometimes given, but not until some time after the raid. Thus it was reported on 15th February that incendiary bombs had "recently" burnt out the interior of the Perse School, at Cambridge. In fact, the raid had been on 16th January. The older part of the building — the assembly hall, library and ten classrooms — had been largely destroyed, and the main hall and some rooms behind it had lost their roofs.

This method of releasing information to the public meant, inevitably, that considerable satisfaction was derived by some people in developing a "grapevine" to feed the general curiosity. A Cambridge undergraduate who was an observer for the Mass Observation organisation conducted his own experiment after one February raid to see how the system worked. He reported:

> Between 11 and 12.30 last night I heard bombs and saw fires over house-tops. That was my only direct experience. I thought it might be interesting to note how the news reached me by word of mouth:
>
> 1. At breakfast, our landlady, prefacing her remark with the usual "It doesn't do to spread these things, so don't let it go any further", reported: "The milkman says it was in X street".
>
> 2. After a lecture, a friend spoke of "a fair-sized blitz", giving some details of location and houses and some industrial premises damaged.

Left: Bomb damage in "an East Anglian town", probably Cambridge, after air raids on the night of 24th February. *Cambridge Daily News*

Right: Fireman fighting fires at the Leys School, Cambridge, after an air raid on 16th January. *Cambridge Daily News*

3. As we stood talking a boy on a bicycle came to report to his mother, a bedmaker at the college, what he had seen. He told her of "17 houses down", and she said to the other woman present: "I like to send him to find out, in case I know any of the poor things there."

4. As I entered the faculty library, the librarian, in his office, pulled a face. He said he lived near a house that had been bombed. He had fled under the table at the whistle of the following bomb, and had been sick through shock. He looked white.

5. In the university library of music the attendant's first words were: "Did you hear the trouble last night?" He then described the bombing of houses in the suburb in which he lived, and detailed the casualties.

6. A friend passing in the street, who had been fire-watching last night, called "Exciting night last night!"

7. At tea, our landlady told a story of a person being turned back from a road cordon and of buses being diverted because of craters.

8. During the evening a friend in the street discussed the difficulties of digging up bodies!

Submitting this report on everyday human behaviour to the Mass Observation office, the undergraduate reported that he had "deliberately refrained from asking questions in all the above cases and confined my comments to 'yes' and 'no'."

There were times when the authorities were seriously concerned about public behaviour after raids, although the problems never assumed serious proportions. Looting, for example, was almost unknown, although there was one prosecution at Ipswich in June, when a seventeen-year-old Leicester youth was sent to prison for six months for looting a bomb-damaged home. The more common complaint was of simple "nosiness"; the *Eastern Daily Press* published in May a strong editorial criticism of sightseers who travelled to view air raid damage. The local Royal Society for the Prevention of Cruelty to Animals was concerned that some people gave inadequate attention to the cats and dogs who lost their homes.

The raids were ever present in people's minds, even when they had no more

serious consequences than loss of sleep and discomfort. Some people went to public shelters, but they were not popular, and many of the brick surface shelters hurriedly built when the war started were by 1941 judged to be unsafe. Even if safe, they were bare and cold. Many schools had shelters of this kind and in January, 1941, the Norwich City Council had tried to persuade the Board of Education to equip them with electric heaters. Some people had steel "Anderson" shelters installed below ground level in their gardens, but these were cold and damp; it had never been intended that people should sleep in them. The majority of people stayed in their own homes, and went into their cellars or crouched under tables or staircases when danger seemed close at hand.

A new type of shelter was made available during 1941 — the "Morrison" tabletop shelter, which was rather like a metal cage with a steel frame 6 feet 6 inches long, 4 feet wide and 2 feet 9 inches high. The top consisted of a steel plate one-eighth of an inch thick, and the sides were of heavy wire mesh. Two adults and two young children could crawl inside and lie down, and it was calculated that they would be safe if two floors of a house collapsed on top. When there were no raids, they could use it as a table! In fact, it occupied so much space in an average room that it left them no choice. One million of these were manufactured and they were issued free to families living within a thousand yards of airfields. In East Anglia special arrangements were made to supply them in some small towns and villages which had been selected by the military as "nodal points" around which defence would concentrate in the event of an invasion. In other areas the Morrison shelters were intended to be a free issue to families whose income did not exceed £350 a year, and to be available to others on payment of £7 12s.6d. But distribution proceeded only slowly.

A young man living in Ipswich, John Rogers, noted in his diary one day in May:

> Felt tired, after a terrible night. Bombs fell all the time. They were pretty close, too. Windows were smashed in our street (He lived in Ivry Street). But we found that we were O.K. We were down the cellar most of the time. Rather scared.

A Mass Observation correspondent, reporting on Ipswich at this time, wrote:

> The siren goes nearly every night, often twice a night, and has done so continually ever since the blitz-raids started. There has never been a lull in the sort of air war that Ipswich has experienced. The fact of the war has been kept in people's minds all the time, and they have very much a front-line mentality, with people evacuated, previously unheard-of numbers of troops in the town and surrounding countryside, and bombers passing overhead every night, to the accompaniment of sirens.[(6)]

In circumstances such as these, daytime gossip had a therapeutic value.

Almost every town and village was visited by the Luftwaffe at some time or another. Most towns suffered considerable damage. Newmarket, for example, had a particularly bad daylight raid on 18th February, when twenty-seven people were killed and 248 injured. The *Ferry Inn* at Horning, one of the best-known East

Servicemen join local civilians in searching the ruins of the *Ferry Inn* at Horning after it had received a direct hit from a bomb on 26th April. Among the many casualties were R.A.F. fighter pilots from an airfield not far away. *George Swain*

Anglian riverside public houses, was bombed on 26th April, and there were many casualties. The Germans attacked many genuine military targets, of course, but much of the bombing was indiscriminate — some of it appeared to be the dumping of bombs after planes had failed to reach their intended targets. Not surprisingly, then, even churches in rural districts were sometimes heavily damaged.

Apart from the bombing, German planes sometimes dived down low enough to machine-gun people on the ground. The *Eastern Daily Press* described on 7th January how a motorist who had had to abandon his car in the countryside when he ran out of petrol one night returned the following day with a friend to collect the vehicle. As they were filling the tank a lone German came down to about 200 feet and opened fire on them. They dived underneath the car and escaped injury. A few days earlier another plane had fired at men working in a stackyard without harming them.

During January there were several machine-gun attacks on trains in various areas. In most cases, little harm was done, but in one attack, on 18th January, two passengers in a train were killed and five others injured. Among the latter was a nineteen-year-old professional pianist, Harold Steward, who lost all the fingers of one hand.

Armed soldiers guard a Junkers Ju.88 which had crash-landed near Somerton, north of Yarmouth, after being damaged by fire from the armed trawler H.M.S. *Galvani,* in peacetime a member of the Hull fishing fleet. *Eastern Daily Press*

Not all the deaths and the damage resulted from deliberate attack by bombs or bullets. Early in the year three elderly women were killed when a crippled R.A.F. bomber crashed on houses in Histon Road in Cambridge. And, of course, the defences did sometimes score hits on German planes, as when A.A. guns brought down a Heinkel bomber at Watton. At the end of January a Junkers Ju. 88 which attacked the armed trawler *Galvani* near Great Yarmouth came off worst in the encounter and flew in from the sea with a wing on fire, crash-landing near the village of Somerton. Covered with mud, the crew of four surrendered cheerfully to their civilian captors, one officer remarking: "We're in good old England at last — we feel at home now". An equally surprising comment came from the pilot of a German bomber brought down near Sudbury; he told the postman to whom he surrendered that things were bad in Germany and that the Nazi army was fed up with the war.

Many individuals acted with great bravery during these raids, and the authorities made a number of awards during 1941 to East Anglian men and women. Two Post Office telephonists who had worked through the air raids at Great Yarmouth and Lowestoft, Miss Beatrice Newby and Miss Dorothy Dallimer, received the British Empire Medal for their "courage and devotion to duty". Two Aldeburgh ladies were awarded the George Medal for their work in the civil defence service during a raid. As must often be the case with the award of such decorations, these awards recognised the qualities of whole bodies of men and women of whom the individuals were chosen representatives.

One of the strangest Luftwaffe visits was made to Debden airfield in Essex on 14th February. A Heinkel He. 111 landed on the runway and taxied towards the control tower, then turned and took off again! If the pilot had made an error, it is difficult to imagine who was most surprised; he or the R.A.F. lads who watched in amazement and failed to act quickly enough to catch him.[7]

So, as we have seen, many civilians in East Anglia felt that they were as much in the front line as many of those who had been called up to serve in the forces. But out in the North Sea, and frequently actually within sight of the East Anglian coast, men's suffering was of a quite different dimension. Early in February, 1941, the Fuhrer, Adolf Hitler, issued a directive that his navy and air force must concentrate on attacking all seaborne traffic bound for the United Kingdom, and all ports of entry. The idea was to starve the British into surrender.

By laying extensive minefields and maintaining constant attacks on convoys, the Germans had a large measure of success, and it was not until mid-summer that the British war chiefs began to think they were getting on top of the problem. A

Mrs Dorothy Clarke, an Aldeburgh ambulance driver, and Mrs Bessie Hepburn, her assistant, who were awarded the George Medal for conspicuous gallantry during an air raid. Their uniforms do not seem to have been normal issue for A.R.P. or civil defence workers; perhaps they made them for themselves.
Eastern Daily Press

great deal of shipping was sunk and, in addition, by the beginning of March there were 2,600,000 tons of damaged shipping waiting to be repaired. The ports had been under heavy attack since the beginning of the winter, but between March and May, 1941, the bombing was stepped up. During May there were German raids on the Merseyside ports on seven successive nights. Sixty-nine out of a hundred and forty-four berths were put out of action and for some time the tonnage which could be handled was reduced to a quarter of normal. On 10th May five of the London docks were badly damaged, with direct hits on seventy-one key points; this was the same raid which caused the destruction of the Chamber of the House of Commons.

The dramatic events which made the big headlines concerned the capital ships engaged in this battle at sea. German auxiliary cruisers, generally converted merchantmen, did much of the damage, but anxieties focused on the battleships

Scharnhorst and *Gneisenau*, which slipped out from Kiel to the North Atlantic and sank twenty-two ships in two months. They then put into Brest, where the British did their best to bottle them up and attack them from the air, with limited success. The "pocket battleship" *Admiral Scheer* and the heavy cruiser *Admiral Hipper* were also a constant threat. The *Scheer* returned to Kiel on 1st April having sunk seventeen Allied vessels; the *Hipper*, during a fortnight's cruise out of Brest in

Booms were laid across the Thames Estuary, the mouth of Harwich harbour and other harbour entrances to prevent U-boats and surface craft gaining access, one of the boom defence depots being at Felixstowe Dock. This photograph shows a boom defence vessel of the *Bar* class laying moorings similar to those to which the destroyer is lying in the illustration on page 9.
East Anglian Daily Times

February, sank seven out of nine ships in an unescorted convoy.

In May there was a climactic sea battle. British air reconnaissance sighted the German battleship *Bismarck* and the heavy cruiser *Prinz Eugen* almost immediately after they had sailed from Gdynia and they were kept under observation as they moved through the Baltic towards the Atlantic, where the British assembled a massive naval force to meet them. The battle cruiser *Hood* and the battleship *Prince of Wales*, with escorts, sailed from Scapa Flow and rendezvoused with the British Home Fleet, consisting of the battleship *King George V*, the aircraft carrier *Victorious* and numerous cruisers and destroyers. On 24th May the battle began.

One of the first shells fired from the *Bismarck* penetrated a magazine on the *Hood* and she exploded, sinking within three minutes; three men were saved, 1,416 were lost. The *Prince of Wales*, although damaged, put several shells into the *Bismarck* and a plane from the aircraft carrier *Victorious* later hit her with a torpedo, but still she did not sink, though her steering gear was damaged. Hemmed in by dozens of ships of the Royal Navy, the *Bismarck* was repeatedly hit by shells from the battleship *King George V* and the battle cruiser *Renown*. Eventually, a torpedo from the cruiser *Dorsetshire* sent Hitler's largest battleship to the bottom, with the loss of 2,100 lives.

Compared with the scale of these events, the war in the North Sea seemed unremarkable. But the harsh reality was that by May, 1941, one vessel was being lost every other day, despite the fact that the number of convoys was severely restricted.[8] In the area just off Lowestoft alone, four vessels were sunk within three weeks during May, the trawlers *Ben Gairn* and *King Henry* and the drifters *Uberty* and *Thistle*.

The little ships of the Royal Naval Patrol Service had virtually no protection against attack from the air by the cannon and machine-guns of the marauding Junkers Ju.88s: usually just a small steel box behind the wheelhouse, with a peephole through which the skipper could keep observation during an attack.

Sometimes disaster took the form of collision in the pitch blackness of a winter night. One such disaster occurred just off Harwich on 20th September when a patrol of small vessels coming out from Ipswich at full speed found themselves under attack from enemy planes. In the general confusion one of them rammed the minesweeping trawler *Marconi*, which was moored to a buoy. The *Marconi*'s engine room began to flood rapidly and the order was given to abandon ship. At that point, one of the German planes dropped three bombs in a line alongside the doomed vessel. An indication of the degree to which seamen became inured to their life of hardship and danger — or perhaps an indication of the extent of their exhaustion — is given by the fact that during a last-minute check one stoker was found fast asleep in his bunk! All the crew escaped on to a raft, and then into a boat; as they rowed away the *Marconi* created such suction as she disappeared below the surface that one of the oars snapped under the strain.

Later in the year there was an even worse loss a little further north. H.M.S. *Umpire*, a new submarine making her first voyage, was on her way from Chatham to the Clyde for trials, sailing on the surface in a convoy of merchant ships, escorted by minesweeping vessels. Off the Norfolk coast *Umpire* developed engine trouble and parted company with the convoy, one motor launch remaining with her for company. It was a calm but pitch black night, but there was a ban on showing any lights. At about midnight the northbound convoy was due to pass another one sailing south. They should have passed, according to the law of the sea, port-to-port, but this did not happen, and the consequence was that soon afterwards the lookouts on the *Umpire* suddenly discerned the southbound convoy coming head-on towards their vessel. The captain ordered the submarine to alter course, and the lookouts saw half a dozen vessels slip past to starboard. Then there was another vessel almost on the submarine's bows; as he ordered hard-a-port, *Umpire*'s captain knew that a collision was inevitable. The *Umpire* was struck by the escort trawler *Peter Hendricks* and sank in thirty seconds. Two officers and two lookouts were picked up, but the rest of the crew, two officers and twenty men, were drowned.

It would be possible to relate many such stories, for such disasters were almost commonplace. The heroism of those whose duty it was to try to keep open these vital sea lanes was of a special quality unlikely ever to be surpassed.

Naturally, the East Coast lifeboats were regular participants in the dangers, and their crews showed similar courage. Coxswain Henry Blogg, of Cromer, who was sixty-five, became the archetypal hero and was three times awarded the Gold Medal of the Royal National Lifeboat Institution. The way in which he won the third award graphically illustrates the bravery of such men.

In the early hours of 6th August Convoy FS559 was finding its way along the Norfolk coast in conditions which, for that time of year, were appalling: a dark moonless night, with squalls of wind and rain, so that visibility was almost nil, and with heavy seas running. Two destroyers and some armed trawlers were keeping the merchantmen company. Suddenly, unexpectedly, six of the ships touched bottom, and within minutes they were bumping dangerously on the hard sand as big waves hit them. One of them, the *Paddy Hendly*, was on her maiden voyage. The others were the steamers *Taara*, *Oxshott*, *Gallois*, *Deerwood* and *Aberhill*. They had run aground on the Haisborough Sands, east-north-east of Cromer.

The news reached Cromer just after 8 a.m. and the lifeboat *H.F. Bailey* put to sea. At the scene of the disaster, the situation was grim. A whaler from one of the escorting destroyers had managed to take off most of the crew of the *Taara*, but twelve men had been lost in other rescue attempts. Only the masts, funnel and upperworks of the *Oxshott* were still above water. The six stricken vessels lay close together, "in steep breaking seas in which it was not to be expected that any boat could live", as an Admiralty report later recounted. Very soon only the bridge of the *Deerwood* could be seen, the *Taara* lay with her back broken, both bow and stern under water, and the *Aberhill* and *Paddy Hendly* had also had their backs broken.

Blogg first went to investigate the *Oxshott*, which was clearly in danger of breaking up. He found sixteen men roped together, hanging on to the superstructure. There was no way of getting a line to them. Then Blogg spotted a gap in the shattered superstructure of the vessel into which he thought it might be possible to drive the bow of the lifeboat. This was a desperately dangerous manoeuvre, for it meant going in over the submerged deck of the *Oxshott* and ramming the lifeboat's fender against the torn plates of the bigger vessel, which might have jagged edges that, with the firece motion of the sea, would cut like a

The Cromer lifeboat *H. F. Bailey* in which Coxswain Henry Blogg and the Cromer lifeboatmen went to the assistance of Convoy FS559 on 6th August. *R.N.L.I.*

saw. There were moments of crisis; twice the lifeboat bumped heavily on the *Oxshott*'s deck beneath it, several times the seas broke over it and washed it back from its precarious position. But eventually all sixteen men were rescued.

The Cromer lifeboat then turned to the *Gallois*. It was still above water and Blogg was able to hold the lifeboat alongside while thirty-one crewmen jumped aboard or came down ropes. Now getting overcrowded, the lifeboat made its way to a destroyer in nearby deep water and transferred the rescued seamen. By this time two other lifeboats were on the scene: the number two boat from Cromer, the *Harriot Dixon*, and the Gorleston lifeboat *Louise Stephens*. The *Harriot Dixon* went to the *Taara* and, using tactics similar to those Blogg had adopted with the *Oxshott*, took eight men off and transferred them to a destroyer. The *Louise Stephens*, meanwhile, rescued the twenty-three crew of the *Aberhill*.

Blogg and his men in the *H.F. Bailey* turned their attention to the *Deerwood*, on which nineteen crewmen were assembled on the bridge, the only part above water. Again Blogg took the lifeboat in over the submerged deck and held her against the superstructure while the men clambered on board. The *H.F. Bailey* then visited the *Aberhill* and the *Taara*, found the other lifeboats already handling those situations, and so went on to the sixth vessel, the *Paddy Hendly*, and took off twenty-two men. Then, at last, with forty-one rescued seamen on board, she made for Great Yarmouth.

But the day's work was not yet done. A wrecked trawler was sighted and investigated, but there was nobody on board. The *H.F. Bailey* was then hailed by a destroyer, which took the forty-one seamen on board and sent the lifeboat to a minesweeping trawler, from which two bodies were taken ashore. Then, at 5 p.m., nine hours after leaving Cromer, a badly-damaged *H.F. Bailey* entered the harbour at Great Yarmouth. It had saved eighty-eight men that day.

Coxswain Henry Blogg at work on a crab pot. When this photograph was taken in 1941 he was a man of sixty-five and had been coxswain of the Cromer lifeboat for more than thirty years. *R.N.L.I.*

Henry Blogg received the third service clasp to his R.N.L.I. Gold Medal, and the British Empire Medal as well; these were among seven medals, eighteen citations on vellum, and £117 in cash awarded to Norfolk lifeboat crews for their efforts on 6th August on Haisborough Sands. Before these awards could be presented in the autumn by the Third Sea Lord, the Cromer lifeboat had figured in another spectacular episode in which Coxswain Blogg and six of his crew had been washed overboard from the *H.F. Bailey*. They were trying to approach a steamer which had run aground on Hammond Knoll, quite close to the scene of the August adventure. A full north-east gale was blowing and when the lifeboat was 100 yards from the steamer, a huge wall of water overwhelmed it and spun it over until the keel came out of the water. Blogg was picked up and immediately resumed command, steering the lifeboat to each of the six men still in the water. Pulling them on board was a difficult business, and it was twenty-five minutes before the last of them, Edward Walter Allen, was rescued from the icy water. He did not survive; at the inquest it was said that he had been in bad health for years, yet was always ready to join the lifeboat crew.

Apart from these hazardous missions to stricken vessels in the North Sea, the East Coast lifeboatmen were regularly called out to pick up airmen whose planes had ditched. The Walton-on-Naze boat *E.M.E.D.*, for example, was called out seven times for this purpose during 1941, though only once returning with a body.

During the autumn the Sheringham lifeboat rescued five Polish airmen from a Wellington bomber which came down off the Wash, after they had spent seventeen hours drifting in a rubber dinghy, and the Wells lifeboat, collaborating with an R.A.F. air-sea rescue launch, picked up six airmen from another crashed Wellington.

The Walton lifeboat was kept busy for more than a fortnight early in the year when a Swedish steamer, the *Belgia*, caught fire and drifted on to the beach at Frinton. First she helped to take out firemen and pumps to fight the fire from the seaward side, then later she stood by on several days while tugs tried to pull the vessel off. Finally, she took off the salvage crew when the ship was taken in tow to Harwich. Another unusual job a few days later involved taking naval ratings out to destroy a mine which was floating about a mile off Walton — which they did with a machine-gun.

Apart from the enemy planes overhead, the explosions frequently heard from the coast, and the arrival of injured seamen in local hospitals, the civilian population did not have much direct experience of the war at sea. But there were occasional unpleasant reminders, as when, in the words of a local diarist, Mrs Sarah Williams:

> Everywhere in Sheringham was pervaded by a pungent smell of oil today. We discovered at dinner-time that it was due to a sinking oil tanker lying off the coast. I heard that it was due to (1) an English mine, (2) a German mine, (3) a torpedo, and (4) a bombing attack.

In these various ways, the early months of 1941, as experienced by the people of East Anglia, was a deeply depressing period. The enemy seemed to be having things very much his own way. His planes were doing great damage to targets on land and at sea, and the British response was clearly limited by absence of adequate resources.

The German attempt at blockade had been sufficiently effective to cause a considerable tightening of the belt, as rationing became more severe. The East Anglian regiments of the Army and many others were being shunted around the country, completing their training, but without any clear indication of how they were to be deployed. From the war fronts overseas the news was mixed: successes in North and East Africa, but setbacks in the Balkans and grave problems in maintaining supply lines in the Mediterranean.

In these desperate circumstances, the national will showed no sign of faltering, and the Prime Minister, Winston Churchill, could be confident of the response he would evoke when, in June, he broadcast to the nation:

> We are resolved to destroy Hitler and every vestige of the Nazi regime. From this nothing will turn us—nothing. We will never parley, we will never negotiate with Hitler or any of his gang. We shall fight him by land, we shall fight him by sea, we shall fight him in the air until, with God's help, we have rid the earth of his shadow and liberated its peoples from his yoke.

CHAPTER THREE

Defending Homes and Workplaces

NEITHER government, defence organisations nor public sat idle while the punishment was inflicted. Efforts to improve the British war machine, which had been well in hand at the turn of the year, were steadily developed.

So far as East Anglia was concerned, the apex of the defence organisation was the Regional War Room which had been established in a large house called St Regis in Montague Road, Cambridge. Since 1st June, 1940, this had been the centre of operational control, in constant communication with the commanding officers of service units in the region, with the police and fire service, with A.R.P. Controllers, with local authorities, and also with all relevant government departments in London. In many cases the local A.R.P. Controllers were police superintendents or senior officers of the local authority.(1)

After the raids in the early months of winter in 1940, the A.R.P. services were becoming battle-hardened. Their basic organisation was sound: there was a network of control centres, manned by full-timers, a series of specialist units — rescue, casualty, and decontamination — and a force of volunteer part-time wardens covering every street or other appropriate sector.

The big German fire-raids at the end of 1940 revealed a basic weakness. In a major reorganisation, the A.R.P. service became the Civil Defence services, and in August, 1941, the 1,600 local fire brigades of all sorts and sizes were incorporated into a new National Fire Service. Large water storage tanks were set up wherever suitable sites could be found in built-up areas, most of them of 5,000 gallons capacity, and every householder was exhorted to have buckets of water and/or sand ready to hand.

In January, 1941, the Home Secretary gave notice that some form of compulsory firefighting force must be created.(2) Before the government had had time to introduce the necessary measure, most towns in East Anglia were already recruiting volunteers. Public meetings were organised, thousands of leaflets were distributed, and in some areas wardens did a door-to-door canvass. A meeting at Earlham Fiveways, Norwich, on 5th January was typical: most of the hundred local residents who attended volunteered on the spot. A week or so later at Bury St Edmunds a similar meeting produced three dozen volunteers, and a comparable response was seen almost everywhere. Many firms also took action before compulsion was introduced. The Eastern Counties Omnibus Company, for example, placed bags of sand on all vehicles and gave drivers and conductors firefighting training during January. But still this was not enough. The local newspapers were full of appeals for more people to come forward more enthusiastically.

From February, under the terms of a new Fire Regulation, all males between the ages of eighteen and sixty, except those who were already serving in the Home Guard or Civil Defence, became liable to forty-eight hours unpaid service each month. In those areas where the new regulations were immediately put into effect, firefighting parties of at least three men had to be on duty continuously, seven days a week, twenty-four hours a day, at all business premises, shops, factories, public buildings and schools. Each party had to be equipped with a minimum of one stirrup pump, one crowbar, two "receptacles" filled with water, and two bags of sand.

Firefighting parties went on look-out duty when the sirens sounded an "Alert". At other times, they were on stand-by, which meant they could "get their heads down" on canvas beds during any nocturnal hours which were undisturbed by raiders. Most men naturally preferred to be in their own beds at home, with their families. Fire-party duty had no glamour, and it was not popular, as two entries in the diary of young Ipswich factory worker John Rogers indicate:

> My fire-watching again. Went on duty at 9.30 pm and played darts until nearly midnight. Lucky with warnings — one crash, no sirens . . .

The second entry, referring to a Saturday afternoon duty, indicates a problem that arose:

> Fire-watching at business from 3 to 5 o'clock. The boss asked me to take his place – what could I say?

Eventually there were some prosecutions of those who failed to turn out, as in Norwich in July when two men were each fined £1.

The authorities wanted street fire parties to protect residential property, but this was more difficult to arrange. Volunteers were still slow to come forward, and there was not yet enough equipment to go round. The stirrup pump was the essential item. It was rather like the pump used by many gardeners; one part was placed in a bucket of water and the whole thing was steadied by the foot as it was hand-pumped; a second person directed the jet of water on to the fire; and a third replenished the bucket of water. Until these pumps came through in adequate numbers, many fire bombs were tackled with a spade, or even a domestic shovel, with which they were scooped up and thrown into a bucket of sand or, if possible, on to an open space where they would do no harm.

The authorities issued detailed advice on "How to tackle fire bombs":

> When fire bombs fall indoors or where they can start a fire, they should be tackled resolutely and at once. As some will contain high explosive, always take best available cover. Leave all fire bombs alone if they fall where they can do no particular harm.

Norwich A.R.P. Committee produced a stiff card, printed on both sides,

East Anglian Daily Times

WITH WHICH IS INCORPORATED THE "IPSWICH EXPRESS" (ESTABLISHED 1839).

No. 22,569 . . IPSWICH, WEDNESDAY, JANUARY 1, 1941 Price 1½d.

HITLER THANKS HIS SOLDIERS

FIRE WATCHERS FOR EVERY FACTORY, SHOP AND HOUSE

GOVERNMENT TO INTRODUCE PROTECTION ON COMPULSORY PRINCIPLE

EVERYBODY'S DUTY TO GUARD HOMES AND WORK PLACES

" THE QUESTION OF FIRE-FIGHTING IS MOST URGENT "

SHIP LOSSES BELOW AVERAGE

NAZIS FOR ONCE FAIL TO EXAGGERATE

which could be hung up prominently in the home. The guidance given was fairly basic: buckets of water and sand or earth should be kept where they were quickly accessible, but where the sand would keep dry; if one left one's home for any appreciable period of time, gas and electricity supplies should be cut off, windows should be left uncurtained, and keys should be deposited with the street warden.

By the end of the winter civil defence arrangements had greatly strengthened and improved in most respects. But there were still not sufficient uniforms and equipment for everyone. During the winter of 1940-41 most civil defence personnel had been issued with nothing more than blue cotton overalls, which they wore over their own warm clothing. The W.V.S. supplied them with some knitted clothing, but it was high summer before the issue began of proper battle-dress uniforms of blue serge, with overcoats, berets and boots. Many of the civil defence depots and wardens' posts were uncomfortable and without proper sleeping accommodation — and often they were unsafe.

The way in which the victims of the air raids were dealt with was also largely a matter of improvisation. It was the middle of the year before a full network of "rest centres" could be created, in which the bombed-out could find temporary refuge. It was not until August that emergency feeding arrangements were in place, with kitchens in schools and halls, operated by the local authorities under the direction of the Ministry of Food.

"First-aid" repairs to damaged property represented an enormous task, but they were carried out expeditiously, so that families could return to their homes, even if they had windows boarded up and roofs covered with tarpaulins. On 5th May the War Damage Commission opened an office in the County Bowling Club in Cambridge to deal with compensation claims from the whole of the East Anglia region.

The defence of some factories and industrial installations called for more elaborate arrangements. Camouflage paint was freely splashed about, but ports, munitions factories and airfields needed something more. The attempt to safeguard them against attack included the building of dummy installations and airfields. Those intended to represent industrial or commercial areas were designated "SD sites" and "Starfish", those made to look like airfields were "K-sites" and "Q-sites".

One Q-site was near the village of Bucklesham, a few miles east of Ipswich, between Nacton crossroads and Levington Bridge. In the early summer of 1941 the Army took over a 32-acre field. When the tenant farmer arrived one morning to look over his crops, he found a sentry barring his way and "over most of my field an assortment of tarpaulin-covered objects". He was not allowed in. The Army's plan was to erect light structures to suggest oil tanks, cranes and other port installations to decoy raiders from the real port of Ipswich, which was to be protected by a

MAJOR'S CORNER
FORD Depot: PRINCES ST. ('Phone 3744) IPSWICH

EVERY HOUSEHOLDER'S WAR WEAPON

'Belling' BOMB SNUFFER

TRIED and proved under actual bombing conditions, this Bomb Snuffer is a combination of the dustbin lid and the sandbag. It gives protection against explosion because the Snuffer is used as a shield between you and the bomb. It cuts off the intense light, heat and flame, stops the spitting of molten metal, prevents the bomb spreading further fires and eventually extinguishes it. Simply pick it up on the end of a pole or strong broom handle (hook supplied) and drop it over the bomb, when the contents of dry sand immediately fall on the bomb and smother it. It is the easiest and safest way of applying sand to an incendiary bomb. Any man or woman can use it. Requires only one person to operate, nothing to get out of order. No house or building should be without at least one of these simple appliances for controlling incendiary bombs.

Obtainable through any Electrical Shop or Ironmonger.

PRICE EACH 12/6
(FREE OF PURCHASE TAX)

WRITE *also for descriptive folder of these other 'Belling' War-time necessities:*

Baby Cooker £4/19/6 (Plus 27½%) Tax Extra
Bed Warmer 24/- (Plus 33⅓%) Tax Extra
Boiling Rings from 19/- (Plus 33⅓%) Tax Extra
Champion Heaters from 24/- (Plus 33⅓%) Tax Extra

BELLING & CO. LTD., BRIDGE WORKS, ENFIELD, MIDDLESEX

C.R.C.78

R.A.F. DANCE ORCHESTRA'S
UR OF SUFFOLK VILLAGES

STOLE SERVICE BLANKETS
IPSWICH MAN

A bucket of sand was officially suggested as the most effective way of smothering an incendiary bomb, but many commercial firms introduced their own refinements, as this advertisement from the *East Anglian Daily Times* shows. To discourage the use of simple remedies the Germans fitted many incendiary bombs with a 3½ oz. explosive charge in an extension to the nose; this was detonated after a delay of up to seven minutes.

A Heinkel He.111 which crash landed in a field at Waterend Farm, Ovington, on 18th February. It had flown into three cables dangling below parachutes fired by rocket from the R.A.F. airfield at Watton; this defensive device was officially known as PAC (parachute and cable). *Eastern Daily Press*

smoke screen, but the effort that went into it was never justified, and within a year the whole thing had been removed.*

There was another such site, intended to protect Brightlingsea. The Admiralty devised an elaborate installation on the marshes; ditches were dug and a tank set up in such a way that it could release oil into the ditches, which could then be ignited by a small explosive charge. The resulting blaze over an extensive area was intended to deceive the enemy into believing that he had hit his target. This plan was never realised, but one day men scything the grass on the site set the whole thing off when they accidentally cut a cable.[3]

Colchester railway station was another potential target which was provided with a decoy site, situated just east of the town between Great Bromley and Great Bentley. The works engineer of Davey, Paxman and Company was put in charge of the installation. Two or three men spent their nights in a dug-out on the site pulling lamps to and fro along wire cables to simulate the lights of locomotives in a shunting yard. In most cases heavy anti-aircraft guns were installed close to these sites.

Decoy sites near important R.A.F. stations served their purpose. Film studio technicians at Shepperton created dummy aircraft, using wood and canvas over a metal frame (it needed one and a half tons of steel for a dummy Wellington bomber). They turned out convincing replicas of planes of all types — so convincing, in fact, that special precautions had to be taken to deter R.A.F. pilots from landing at these sites. The R.A.F. established a Camouflage and Decoy Unit, based initially at Cavenham near Bury St Edmunds; the dummy planes were painted by members of this unit, positioned well away from the areas needing

*In January 1941 the War Cabinet set up a "Committee on Smoke Protection" and much effort and manpower went into this project during the year.

protection, and moved around after German planes had been overhead. Enormous ingenuity and effort went into these operations, as the following recollection by one of those involved, Mr Percy Bested, shows:

> We were taken into one of the hangars (at Duxford) where, hidden beneath a huge tarpaulin, was a cleverly adapted vehicle resembling a real plane. It had folding wings and was fitted with all the appropriate lighting both on wings and tail. There was only one entry — the driver's door, made of armoured plate. Once you were in you were in, and it was no use suffering from claustrophobia. The only view was through an aperture cut out of the armour plate that took the place of the usual windscreen.
> After receiving instructions and a demonstration, I was ordered to drive this unusual vehicle to a "Q-site" between Linton and Horseheath, where I was greeted with a few cheers on my arrival.
> During daylight hours we would tow into the woods at the edge of the field all the dummy planes, and shift other pieces of equipment, leading the Germans — should they be taking photographs from the air — to think the planes had taken off on a mission. This action was regularly repeated.
> At night, we would be alerted if the Germans were in the area and I or my mate would be instructed to drive our special plane up the fully-lit flarepath twelve times in succession. This gave the Germans to believe a squadron of planes was taking off for action . . .
> It conned the Germans. One night I had driven up the flarepath when suddenly the darkness was turned to the brightness of day. They bombed us continually with incendiaries. A few miles away at Eversden we had a site called a Starfish where, immediately the Germans bombed us, they commenced lighting huge fires. This happened on several occasions, convincing the Germans they had caused untold damage to either Cambridge or one of the surrounding R.A.F. stations.[4]

R.A.F. stations which had decoy sites, given in brackets, were: Bircham Newton (Coxford Heath), Duxford (Horseheath), Feltwell (Lakenheath), Honington (Thetford), Marham (Swaffham), Martlesham Heath (Hollesley Heath), Mildenhall (Cavenham), Wattisham (Boxford), Watton (North Tuddenham) and West Raynham (Fulmodestone). All these decoy sites had flare-paths. Wittering and Wyton bases had partial installations, without the flare-paths. Stradishall and Sutton Bridge had decoy flare-paths only.

The anti-aircraft guns around R.A.F. stations and decoy sites occasionally brought down one of the raiding planes, as at Honington when a Junkers Ju.88 crashed near one of the hangars.

With the incessant threat from the air, the blackout was rigorously imposed on civilians. Most householders had by this time either lined their curtains with opaque material or had made up "blackout screens" which they fitted at their windows at dusk and removed next morning. If the smallest chink of light escaped, the wardens rapped on the door to give a warning. The newspapers regularly reported the prosecution of those who had been repeatedly careless — fines of between half a crown and £7 were customary. When a light was shown at the Colchester Playhouse, the employee responsible was fined ten shillings and the manager £1. It was considered a particularly serious offence to allow a bonfire to blaze after dark, and a Thrigby man was fined £20 at Flegg Petty Sessions because of a fire in his stack-yard. When at the end of February a Braintree hotelier was fined £10 for his third blackout offence within ten months, the magistrates warned him that he would be sent to prison if he transgressed again.

An article in the *Bury Free Press* on 11th January sought to educate the public. Pre-war experiments, it asserted, had shown that motor-car lights could be seen from a plane flying at 10,000 feet while it was seven or eight miles away. Even a pocket torch would show up at 6,000 feet to a pilot of a plane three miles away. Villages had certainly been bombed as a direct result of lights being shown, the paper declared.

Vehicles were, of course, required to have lights, but they had to be screened.

Men of the Northamptonshire Regiment erecting tubular steel scaffolding on Clacton beach to prevent the landing of tanks. In the background of this picture, taken in July, can be seen a martello tower, an anti-invasion fortification of an earlier era. *Imperial War Museum*

Ironically, while many drivers were prosecuted for showing too much light, in Cambridge, a town swarming with cyclists, there was a regular round-up by the police of those who rode without lights.

The blackout made life more dangerous. Fatal accidents increased by forty per cent in the first fifteen months of the war. Pedestrians out after dark were urged to wear light-coloured clothes, white when possible. A good deal of criticism was heard of the way some Army vehicles were driven. The chairman of the Yarmouth Bench, fining a soldier for speeding, remarked in April: "There have been so many complaints of Army men exceeding the limit." The Bury St Edmunds coroner declared that there were far too many accidents involving Army vehicles. St Faiths and Aylsham R.D.C. complained to the Chief Constable of Norfolk about the speed of military vehicles in its area, and the *Eastern Daily Press* published an editorial advising the military authorities to take action to improve driving standards.

The fact was that during that long bleak winter when there was very little positive action to engage the servicemen stationed in East Anglia, they were not universally popular with the civilian residents. Reactions varied between town and country. Thus, a Mass Observation reporter found that in Ipswich:

> The presence of soldiers from other parts of the country has had a livening effect on the local life. The influx has, on the surface at any rate, altered the appearance of the town, bringing to it a brighter night life and a more military outlook than it had before.[5]

But from an unidentified East Suffolk village there was a very different report:

> The main grouse seemed to be of a destructive mass of soldiers billetted in the district. "They put them in a nice place and let them spoil it, then they say it's unfit and give them somewhere else to spoil. They are cutting down the trees to make way for the guns and digging up for the tank-traps. I've never seen such a mess".[6]

Although the acute threat of imminent invasion had been removed by the winter weather, anti-invasion defences were still being constructed all over East Anglia, and full-scale exercises took place from time to time, involving the services, the police, and the civil defence forces.

The Regional Commissioner, Sir Will Spens, issued advice on 1st March on how civilians should behave if the Nazis put in an appearance: essentially, they were told to "Stay put". Vehicles were to be immobilised by removing the distributor head, or even smashing the distributor if necessary, and then emptying the petrol tank and puncturing it. This guidance was quickly followed up by various individuals in authority. At a meeting of Wayland R.D.C. on 31st March, for example, a Home Guard officer, Major E.M. Steward, declared that every parish should set about becoming self-contained and self-supporting. Each one, he said, should appoint its own food controller, A.R.P. chief, first-aid commandant, and so on. In the case of an emergency, administrative powers would be delegated to parish committees. The major was obviously speaking to an official brief, for very

Some people donned their gas masks when tear gas was released in a exercise in London Street, Norwich, in October; scores of shoppers just dived into the shops to escape the gas.
Eastern Daily Press

soon thereafter these parish invasion committees were created everywhere, and most of them issued very detailed guidance to their local residents.

> You must read and reread this letter and discuss it with your neighbours until you have a perfectly clear picture in your mind of what we may be in for,

wrote the chairman of the parish invasion committee at Stoke-by-Clare and Wixoe, in West Suffolk. He listed some of the things they might "be in for":

> (a) Parachutists might be dropped near the village, when they would be engaged by the Home Guard.
>
> (b) Heavy bombing might take place, in the hope of interrupting communications or even of driving the population into flight along the roads.
>
> (c) A gas screen might be laid down, with the same purpose.
>
> (d) An initial enemy success might bring the actual fighting into the locality.
>
> (e) The advance of our own troops along the roads towards the coast might interrupt all communications with the rest of the county.
>
> We are warned by the authorities that in any of these cases the district might be thrown back entirely on its own reserves for a period, which they put at a week to a fortnight at the outside.

In about 2,500 words of text, the stark facts of what would follow any of the above events were spelt out to the villagers. If roads were destroyed "every able-bodied man must be prepared to turn out, if called on, taking with him his wheelbarrow, pick and shovel (if he has them) and any other tools that may be useful . . ." If fighting seemed likely to spread to the village itself, "not to mince matters, our own people may find it necessary to destroy houses so as to secure a clear line of fire . . ." As for food supplies, the Parish Food Organiser would "have full power to requisition live animals, eggs, vegetables and other commodities from traders and farmers and from private owners . . ." If there were casualties, and the parish was isolated, "the injured may have to be cared for on the spot for some days by the people of Stoke and Wixoe themselves . . ." And there was a solemn reminder to go nowhere without a gas mask and to "keep a supply of anti-gas Ointment No 2 always at hand and know how to use it — it costs sixpence at any chemists".

In the early weeks of 1941 it was noticeable that not many people were carrying their gas masks with them, as they had been advised to do. Jenny Carr, attending her local W.E.A. class in Norfolk, noted when the tutor was overcome by fumes from the tortoise stove in the room that not one member of the class had a mask. Later in the year, in Ipswich, a Mass Observation representative found:

> Out of a thousand people — approximately equal numbers of men and women — only 3½ per cent were carrying masks, the men slightly more than the women.[7]

During February the newspapers carried a report that the United States

These A.R.P. workers at Cambridge adopted a forceful method of urging people to carry their gas masks; "Don't cry when it's too late" said one of their placards.
Cambridge Daily News

government had warned Britain that the Germans were preparing to use gas as a weapon, and thereafter there was constant publicity about the danger. Photographs were published which suggested that the masks were not uncomfortable or inhibiting when worn; for example, the *Norfolk and Norwich Weekly Press* showed members of the York Bowls Club at Norwich playing a match wearing their masks. Gas rehearsals took place in most towns, wardens hurrying round with rattles and everyone in the streets being urged to put on their masks immediately. It was reported that in one such test, in London Street, Norwich, ninety-eight per cent of the public were well prepared. Small children, even babies, were put into masks from time to time, to get them used to the experience. Sarah Williams, living in Sheringham, had a young son and she confided to her diary:

> Timothy was very upset today because his teacher had arranged for them to go into a gas chamber to test their gas masks. He went, and enjoyed it, and was delighted to find that his gas mask really did work.

In April the Ministry of Home Security issued a leaflet "What to do about Gas". After offering advice — "Put on your gas mask at once . . . Get into any nearby building . . . Go upstairs if the building is a tall one . . . Close all windows . . . Cover your skin up . . ." — it concluded: "We can beat gas attacks — if we know what to do, and do it." Happily, gas was never used.

As well as a gas mask, the one other thing every civilian was supposed to keep with him or her was an identity card. In June a correspondent wrote to the *Eastern Daily Press* complaining he had been refused admission to Norwich Castle Museum because he could not produce his card. He suggested that a list should be published of all public buildings barred to those who did not produce an identity card. Public remonstrances poured down upon him. At Bury St Edmunds, at about the same time, a woman was prosecuted for failing to carry her card. Later in the year the police sometimes made spot checks, and at Flegg Petty Sessions five women were fined from £1 to £4 each after they had been found to be carrying borrowed identity cards when questioned on a Norwich-bound bus.

Concern about spies, which was widespread earlier in the war, had diminished in 1941, but there was a brief flurry of excitement in Cambridge in April, when the decomposed body of a man was found in an air raid shelter. The facts were concealed at the time, but he was in fact a German agent — a twenty-seven-year-old Dutchman called Jan Willen Ter Braak, who had been parachuted into England in the previous November, had failed to make contact with the address he had been given, and had crept into the shelter on Christ's Pieces to commit suicide.

In June, 1940, a very large area of East Anglia extending twenty miles inland from the coast had been declared a defence area and visitors had been banned. This helped to keep out "fifth column" elements, but was primarily intended to minimise the problems of the Army as it constructed physical defences — armed pillboxes, minefields and tank traps — and set explosive charges beneath bridges,

Cambridgeshire A.R.P. and A.F.S. messengers marched to Cambridge Guildhall on 7th July to receive their Colours from the Mayor, Mr E. O. Brown. Afterwards they marched through Cambridge behind their band, said to have been the first of its kind in the United Kingdom.
Cambridge Daily News

and also to give maximum freedom of movement to the very large numbers of troops. In December the defence area was reduced to a five-mile coastal strip and Ipswich and Colchester were excluded from it, but the whole length and breadth of East Anglia continued to be required for the defence-in-depth strategy which had been adopted.

A plan had been drawn up in 1940 to evacuate to the Midlands most of the population of the coastal area, including the towns of Lowestoft, Southwold, Aldeburgh and Felixstowe. The Ministry of Home Security circulated to chief constables and town clerks the precise details of how they were to be moved, 800 at a time in special trains, each person permitted to carry only one suitcase and food sufficient for twenty-four hours. The plan was to be put into effect on 1st July, 1940 — but on 27th June the War Cabinet changed its mind and ordered postponement.

Left: Parachute troops preparing to blow open the main doors of Norwich Castle during Exercise Bulldog, a four-day exercise in the Eastern Command area during June. Others got into the castle by scaling the battlements. *Imperial War Museum*

Right: Armed with Lewis guns mounted for anti-aircraft use, two launches of the Wroxham and Ormesby Broads Flotilla patrol the River Bure. *Imperial War Museum*

In the end, about sixty per cent of the population of the towns was persuaded to leave voluntarily.

But the evacuation plan was preserved on ice, as is shown by a minute submitted to the War Cabinet on 25th February, 1941, by Sir John Anderson, the Lord President of the Council. The Commander-in-Chief, Sir John reported, favoured compulsory evacuation during the Spring months; against this should be balanced the serious loss of food production which would result. Sir John recommended, therefore, a new publicity campaign to persuade non-essential workers to leave of their own free will. At the same time, he undertook that the plan for compulsory evacuation would be kept up-dated. The War Cabinet concurred.

Eight months later Churchill called for a new report. He was assured that preparations had been made to evacuate all civilians from coastal areas between the Wash and the Isle of Wight, and from a number of towns, including Ipswich and Colchester. Only the timing remained to be discussed. During the remainder of the year discussion took place, in utmost secrecy, about the amount of warning of an invasion that could be expected, about the order of priority in evacuating the population (mothers and children first), about the time needed to complete evacuation, and about the best way to avoid confusion between troops moving forward and civilians moving back.(8)

The main GHQ Army reserve was held in the East Midlands and north of

London, behind a line which stretched from Canvey Island, in the Thames, north-westward through Cambridge to the Wash. In front of this defence line there were a series of forward "stop-lines", and during 1941 the Army designated, and fortified, a series of "nodal points" which it intended to defend to the last man. They were divided into three classes, according to the length of time each might be expected to hold out. Most of the routine manning of road blocks was left to the Home Guard, while the regular forces were kept ready for rapid movement wherever a threat might develop. Several Army divisions were posted along the coasts of Norfolk, Suffolk and Essex, a mobile anti-tank brigade was held near the Norfolk-Suffolk border, and further back, around Cambridge, there was the 6th Armoured Division. The *Eastern Daily Press* reported that men of the Royal Norfolk Regiment had been recruited early in 1941 into special units to patrol the more remote rural areas, "ready at a moment's notice to race by pedal cycle and Bren carrier to engage enemy parachutists". They were also manning armed motor boats cruising two hundred miles of Broadland waterways. At the outbreak of war the Royal Navy had assumed responsibility for patrolling inland waterways, but a Wroxham and Ormsby Broads Flotilla formed in 1940 had employed troops of a Young Soldier Battalion as gunners, loaders and spotters. By 1941 the Army had taken full charge, and the Broads Flotilla was part of the 18th Division.

A major invasion exercise involving a mock tank battle was organised in late April and early May, with 75,000 troops taking part. Afterwards the Army

Cambridgeshire and Isle of Ely First-Aid Flying Squad parading in front of their van at their first practice turnout in June. With their own cooks, clerks and drivers, such flying squads were able to give help wherever heavy air raids had overstretched local resources. *Cambridge Daily News*

commander had special praise for the Home Guard: "It showed itself capable of exercising considerable effect on enemy operations of an extensive nature," he said. Two months later there was another, larger, exercise extending over four days, involving 170,000 regular soldiers, including parachutists, 20,000 Home Guards, regular police and special constables, and all branches of the civil defence services. The civilian hospitals were called upon to "admit" and "check" several thousand "casualties". Apart from these full-scale manoeuvres, there were frequent exercises in which regular forces mounted mock assaults on a limited area to test the local Home Guard units.

The preparations to resist invasion also included a rapid, though stealthy, development of the so-called "Auxiliary Field Units", which had first been formed after the retreat from Dunkirk in 1940. They were to be the underground resistance movement behind the enemy lines in the event that an invasion force actually landed and advanced inland. During the course of 1941 this organisation recruited many thousands of men and women and became a highly-organised secret network of armed units.[9]

The R.A.F. was also developing its resources and techniques. Duxford was the headquarters of the Air Fighting Development Unit, which examined and assessed captured enemy planes and evaluated new types of Allied aircraft as they came forward from the factories. Stirlings, Halifaxes and Lancasters passed through Duxford and pilots were trained there in evasion tactics when flying them.(10)

From the early months of 1941 there were some American volunteer pilots among those training at Debden, and all over East Anglia there were squadrons formed of airmen who had come to England from the occupied countries. Throughout the year a Czech squadron (No 311) operated from East Wretham, a satellite of Honington. Two Belgian squadrons (Nos 349 and 350) were formed during the year; and there were eight Free French squadrons, and others composed of Dutch, Norwegian and Polish personnel. Ipswich, according to one writer, became "as cosmopolitan as London, Paris, Sydney or New York".(11)

Thus, as 1941 progressed, the strength of the homeland was built up until with the fruits of autumn thoughts could at last be directed to action overseas.

A Czechoslovak bomber crew prepare to set out on a raid in their Vickers Wellington from an East Anglian airfield, probably East Wretham, which was the home of No 311 (Bomber) Squadron in 1941.
East Anglian Daily Times

CHAPTER FOUR

People on the Move

BY 1941 a very large proportion of the population had, for one reason or another, been removed from their normal home and employment environment; the number of people on the move ran into millions. The heavy air raids on London and other ports and industrial centres resulted in renewed efforts to get mothers and young children away into the country, and another drive was made to evacuate schoolchildren from areas of high risk. The first evacuation of London in September, 1939, had been followed within months by a mass drift back to the capital. An elaborate scheme to remove children from East Coast areas when they faced an invasion threat in the summer of 1940 had similarly ended with a large number of them back in their homes.

Lessons had been learnt — the hard way. When another large-scale evacuation was thought necessary, it was decided to move children in groups of limited size, despatched at weekly intervals to specific reception areas, where proper preparations had been made to receive and billet them. There was very little coercion of householders in the reception areas.

There was also an "assisted private evacuation" scheme for families in the coastal areas of East Anglia. Mothers with children, expectant mothers, the aged and infirm, invalids and the blind, and also those who had lost their homes in the raids, were allowed to find their own accommodation in safe areas. If they could do so (often with relatives) they were given free travel vouchers, and those who took them in could claim lodging allowances.

By February, 1941, in Britain as a whole, more than one and a third million had been moved — the highest number of evacuees at any time during the war, except for the first few weeks of September, 1940.(1) All the coastal towns in the Eastern Counties followed this pattern. Felixstowe, for example, had a pre-war population of 13,500, which fell to 5,620 by August, 1940. After that, week by week until the end of the year, the number of residents rose again. But by February the movement had been reversed, and people were leaving fast.

Parties of London evacuees arrived in various towns in East Anglia throughout January, 1941. The movement then subsided for a few weeks, only to resume with larger numbers after a massive raid on London on the night on 10th-11th March which caused 2,000 fires. Things went fairly smoothly in the reception areas — certainly very much better than in August and September, 1939. Seventy-one mothers and children formed the group which was sent to King's Lynn by train on 2nd January; they were met at the station, taken to St James' Boys' School, where they were given refreshments and medically examined, and then settled in various homes in the town. At Bury St Edmunds the Evacuation Officer took over full use of an unoccupied school and adapted it as a "settlement" for two hundred mothers and children; this effort at community living was extolled as an example that might be followed elsewhere.

Elsewhere there were more than sixty evacuees' social clubs in Norfolk alone, fostered by the county's social welfare staff and the Women's Voluntary Service. The founders of a "Mother's Club for Evacuees" in the Thingoe area of West Suffolk explained that "townees find the rural life too quiet", and so they offered a programme of coffee mornings, meetings and other events to liven things up; this scheme was reported to work well. There was more than a hint of patronage, however, in the way some of the arrangements were made and announced. The W.V.S. Centre Secretary in Mitford and Launditch, a rural district of Norfolk centred on Gressenhall, who collected old prams for the use of mothers "from the poorest parts of London" was being practical and seeking to satisfy a real need. But an *East Anglian Daily Times* report on 29th January struck a different note:

> London women evacuated to Suffolk are not going without their fish and chips — thanks to the forethought of the Duchess of Grafton. Realising how much these women would miss their "threepenny and pennorth", the Duchess, assisted by W.V.S. members, started a fish and chip van which tours the villages around Bury St Edmunds.

There were bitter complaints at a meeting of the Hartismere Rural District Council at Eye in January that local people were not being fairly treated. Cases were cited of residents who had undertaken to receive a mother with two children,

Mrs Herbert Musker, wife of Major Musker, Master of the Suffolk Foxhounds and a well-known figure in the hunting world, serving fish and chips to customers from the West Suffolk W.V.S. van in a Breckland village. *East Anglian Daily Times*

Reminiscent of scenes when Scottish farmers arrived in East Anglia with all their farming equipment by train, this photograph shows an entire farm being evacuated to the West Country. Most farmers remained on their farms and made great efforts to increase food production.
East Anglian Daily Times

but who had then been asked to receive in one case a mother and seven children and in another a mother with six children. As these families refused to be separated, an empty cottage had had to be taken over for them, without going through the formal requisitioning procedure. The *Bury Free Press* summed matters up during May in an editorial: Suffolk had done what it could, but some of the evacuees had "not been of the type one would preferably select". The *Cambridge Daily News* struck a similar note when, reporting the arrival of forty-six more evacuees in May, it observed that they were "of a good type", but added the reservation that they were only five and six years old.

The strains were inevitably severe when provincial and rural homes were invaded by families who had usually never been outside the cities, and often the poorest parts of the cities. Proud housewives did not relish sharing their kitchens with strangers. If they refused to do so, however, they had to accept the considerable extra burden of preparing meals for them. Thus, Jenny Carr noted in her diary in March of one Norfolk household:

> Mr A----- exulting today because his wife's relations (evacuees from London since September) have decided to go back for the summer. He is so glad, as he says his wife is being killed by the extra work cooking for them.

The behaviour of some of the London children roused the ire of East Anglians. When two evacuee boys were bound over by the West Suffolk Juvenile Court in June, after they had indecently assaulted a seven-year-old girl, the North-west branch of the Diocesan Moral Welfare Association was outraged; speakers at its meeting argued that the boys should have been whipped. There was, perhaps not surprisingly in the circumstances of the time, quite a lot of juvenile delinquency, much of it petty thieving. At Norwich in June two evacuees — an eleven-year-old boy and a nine-year-old girl — were taken before the juvenile court charged with stealing a chicken coop. They said they had thought it an "old box", in which the girl would be able to keep rabbits. The case was dismissed.

What was less publicised was the extent of the unhappiness of many of the evacuees, taken suddenly from their homes and planted in an alien environment. In one extreme case, in Cambridge in April, a fifteen-year-old lad from Islington hanged himself in a garden shed. There were many cases of neglect of children. A four-year-old boy brought before the Bury St Edmunds Bench had been found sitting on a kerb in the street looking "like a professional beggar". There were tragedies for which responsibility could not be specifically allocated: a four-year-old drowned at Lavenham, a baby suffocated at Bury St Edmunds, and an eight-year-old killed by a collapsing wall while playing in partly-demolished houses at Colkirk, near Fakenham.

On the other hand, many children took to country life with joy and excitement, and were soon assimilated into local society. At Northwold, near Swaffham, an evacuee, Amelia Sellar, was crowned Queen of the May at the annual ceremony at the Norman School. And at Walsingham an Evacuees' Club produced its own play for the local community.

Some residents positively refused to accept evacuees, and some compulsory billeting orders were issued. The Hadleigh Bench during January imposed a £5 fine on a naval officer who had failed to comply with such an order, and when a New Costessey woman appeared at Norwich Shirehall Petty Sessions in March for the same reason the Bench bound her over, saying that as this was the first such offence to come before them they would be lenient, but that they would not be so thereafter. In different parts of East Anglia fines were imposed throughout 1941; as examples, a Mattishall farmer fined £3 for refusing to take in a seventy-two-year-old woman evacuee and an Acton contractor fined £2 for turning away two evacuee mothers with four children.

The *Eastern Daily Press* published a letter during January from "a London mother" which provided a glimpse of the other side of the picture:

> I have been evacuated from London to Norfolk, and I could find nobody to take me in, until my present hostess took my two children and myself into her home. I must say, with the greatest of sincerity, that such hospitality is far to seek. If London mothers could find such homes as I have found, they would all come away from the danger zone.

The government issued a stream of appeals, through the newspapers and radio, using such slogans as "Won't you give them shelter in your home?" and "Caring for evacuees is a national service". Unfortunately, even when everyone was doing his or her best, there were constant irritants. Bunty Carr, writing in her diary at her Norfolk village shop, noted that:

> At about 10.45 p.m. I saw about 30 evacuees going home from the pub, very merry, singing at the tops of their voices, the men pushing the prams and the kids running behind.

Another entry in her diary reads:

> Pestered by evacuees wanting eggs. We only have eight hens and the demand far exceeds the supply. I watch the poor birds carefully and cherish them tenderly, as they perform at threepence a time!

Another complaint was voiced in the *Eastern Daily Press* in January by a village mother. The London County Council, she reported, had sent sweets to evacuee children and they had been given out at school in front of the local children, who received none. "This sort of thing makes the village children turn on the evacuees," she insisted. By way of contrast, a waitress at a Cambridge cafe was fined £2 in February because she under-charged two London evacuees because she thought they looked so poor. Clearly, it was a no-win situation all round.

At Cambridge a representative of the R.S.P.C.A. suggested that those receiving evacuees should also receive pets they chose to bring with them:

> We appeal for all kind people to receive such dogs temporarily in their homes. In many instances, owners would be able to exercise their dogs . . . We ask readers to think of the frightened and lonely animals, and the distress of their owner friend.

The trickle of evacuees into East Anglia continued throughout the early months of the year. The Clerk of the Wayland R.D.C. appealed from his office at Attleborough to parish councillors and ministers to help with the billeting of two hundred more women and children from London who arrived on 31st March. By early April there were nearly 1,000 evacuees living in Diss: nearly 600 "official" evacuees, 222 "unofficial", and 147 who had "privately" evacuated themselves. The council decided to appoint a full-time assistant to the Billeting Officer (at a salary of £3 a week).

Some people had problems caused by the evacuees who had arrived among them, and others were in difficulties because those who should have evacuated themselves refused to go. This was particularly the case in the coastal belt which had been declared a defence area. During the summer of 1940 all schools in the ten-mile-wide coastal area of Essex, Suffolk and Norfolk had been closed and the children had been sent by rail to Wales and the West Midlands. By the beginning of 1941 so many of them had returned that the authorities had no real choice but to reopen the schools.

Notices were posted in churches and public buldings:

> DANGER OF INVASION: Last year all who could be spared from this town were asked to leave, not only for their own safety, but so as to ease the work of the armed forces in repelling an invasion. The danger of invasion has increased and the Government expects all who can be spared, and who have somewhere to go, to leave without delay . . .

The Great Yarmouth Education Committee was greatly exercised with this problem throughout the year. Its clerk told a meeting in April that the Duke of Kent, during a visit he had just made to the town, had strongly advised mothers to send their children away to safe areas. He arranged with the Ministry of Health facilities to send away one school party every week. Members of the committee, discussing the problem, thought that the response might be better if school parties simply moved to safer areas within the county of Norfolk, but the Whitehall view was that, while this was acceptable in individual cases, it was not satisfactory for school groups. Matters were not helped when the newspapers reported in July that an elderly couple who had left their home on the coast to sleep in a farmhouse in an inland village had been killed in their bed by a direct hit by a bomb. After repeated efforts at persuasion had failed, it was decided by the education committees in both Great Yarmouth and Lowestoft that parents who brought children between five and fourteen back into the towns, without informing the committee, should be prosecuted, and that, unless there were special circumstances, children should be directed to reception areas. Even so, the Minister of Home Security, Mr Herbert Morrison, visited the two towns in October to make yet another appeal — in person this time — to parents to keep their children away.

Some other towns seem to have been more successful. A Mass Observation representative who visited Ipswich in September reported that:

> When the first evacuation of children to the Midlands took place in the summer of 1940, only about 10 per cent of the children went. Now there seems to be very few children about, so presumably they have all been moved, officially or not.[2]

Some of the Dominion governments had offered in the period after the Evacuation from Dunkirk in 1940 to accept British schoolchildren as evacuees, and a Children's Overseas Reception Board was set up in London. This scheme caused some controversy, and Winston Churchill was said to look on it unfavourably. To meet criticism that this was a scheme for the children of the well-to-do, it was ruled that three out of every four children who travelled must come from state (rather than private) schools. Even so, very few working-class children seem to have left East Anglia for overseas. Norwich families sent sixty-two children to Canada, and a local M.P., Mr Geoffrey Shakespeare, brought the parents news towards the end of 1941 that they were thriving there; "each had added from twenty to thirty pounds in weight, and between two and three inches in height."

Despite the difficulties, there had been large-scale evacuation of much of the civilian population of the coastal towns, to the extent that most of their local authorities were in serious financial difficulties because of the loss of rate income. At the beginning of 1941 Essex County Council renewed the appeal for government assistance which it had made during 1940. Many shops in the coastal towns were closed and boarded up and, of those which continued in business, some found they had lost so many of their customers that they could not hope to survive. In Great Yarmouth, for example, one of the town's oldest grocery businesses, Clowe's Stores, closed during July, explaining that their customers had been of "the better-off class" and most of them had left the town.

Some inland towns, on the other hand, had benefited from the movement of population. Cambridge was one such. One of the leading property agents reported in January an "unprecedented" demand for properties of all kinds — to rent or purchase. In the *Cambridge Daily News* the advertisement columns showed many vacancies for domestic servants and night watchmen, as well as for shorthand-typists and shop assistants; and it was not thought inappropriate to publish a feature in April on "Spring redecoration of the home".

The "better-off" were, without question, able to escape many of the worst aspects of civilian life in East Anglia at this period.

Many of those who were "on the move" during 1941 acted under compulsion. First, there were the Service units. Of the forty-three divisions of the British Field Army, only four were overseas during the first half of the year. Altogether 1,800,000 of the men who had been called up were stamping their feet in British barracks and camps. As we have already noted, many divisions, particularly the five new armoured divisions, were only at this time getting their equipment. In any case, there would have been insufficient shipping to move them overseas, or to keep them supplied there. An invasion of Britain was still considered enough of a possibility to make the defence of the homeland the absolute priority.

These 1,800,000 troops were very much kept on the move. Those East Anglian regiments which had become part of the 18th Division, for example, were moved southward in April from Scotland. The 4th Suffolks first found themselves billeted in a bleaching mill near Manchester, and a few months later they moved into the town of Hereford. The 5th Suffolks moved from Hawick to a camp near Lord Derby's home at Knowsley Park in Lancashire, then on to Leominster in Herefordshire. The 2nd Suffolks went first to Crewe Hall, in Cheshire, and then to North Wales. Some of the men were used to clear debris after heavy air raids on Liverpool in May, and in September all three battalions helped farmers in

Leicestershire with their harvest. The 1st Suffolks, meanwhile, moved to Arbury Park, near Nuneaton, and later to Lichfield. They found time to produce a tattoo during August which raised £500 to endow a cot in Nuneaton Hospital.[3]

The experience of these regiments was fairly typical of Army life at the time; a great deal of movement, a great many training exercises, and quite a lot of time at leisure, much of it spent at sport. Some of the training was not too arduous; one of the men wrote from Hereford during the summer:

> We amused ourselves one Sunday doing battle with the Home Guard. I rather fancy more eating of buns and drinking of tea was done than fighting the invader, for every time we stopped for a moment or two some kind lass ran out with jugs and plates full of good fare.

But some of the training was arduous, involving movements with motor transport over a very wide area of central England, Lancashire, Yorkshire and Wales.

By this stage of the war all men between the ages of nineteen and forty-one had been called up for service in the armed forces. As they reached the lower age limit, young men were called up in batches; they said farewell to their families and reported for training, and, although accustomed to the idea after many long months

Members of the Women's Home Defence Corps competing with Home Guard personnel on a Cambridge rifle range in October. *Cambridge Daily News*

of war, many of them still found it a shock. John Rogers, when he was forced to leave his job as an assistant in an Ipswich clothing factory, registered his feelings in his diary:

> When the news came through that the 19s would shortly have to register, I was partly stunned. It seemed as if I was in a dream . . . and I would awake to find that the war was just a bad dream. I don't want to go, but will try and make the most of it when I have

KEEP THIS CARD SAFELY

NATIONAL SERVICE (ARMED FORCES) ACTS

Certificate of Registration

Occ. Classn. No. 172 33 .... Registration No. NWL 20472

Holder's Name BREWSTER Lawrence William

Home Address 59. The Close, Ipswich

Date of Birth 27 June 1904

Holder's Signature L W Brewster

READ THIS CAREFULLY

Care should be taken not to lose this certificate, but in the event of loss, application for a duplicate should be made to the nearest office of the Ministry of Labour and National Service.

If you change your address, etc., at any time between the date of registration and the date of being called up for military service, you must complete the appropriate space on the other side of this certificate and post it at once. A new Certificate of Registration will then be sent to you.

If you voluntarily join H.M. Forces you should hand this certificate to the appropriate Service Officer.

You should not voluntarily give up your employment because you have been registered for military service.

This certificate must be produced on request to a constable in uniform.

A person who uses or lends this certificate or allows it to be used by any other person with intent to deceive, renders himself liable to heavy penalties.

N.S.2. Wt. 37642/4471 1000 M 1/41 T. & W. Ltd. A95426 51-8478

A certificate of registration for military service.

> to . . . I thought my chief fears would be that I might be killed. That hardly ever comes to me — my chief "wonder" is how I will get on without those little extras that home life gives . . .

The archetypal recruit, as portrayed at the time in press and on radio, was bursting with enthusiasm to get into the fighting, but this Ipswich lad may more accurately have reflected the real mood.

Now the time had come to draw young women into the net of war activity. On 19th April all women aged twenty-one (that is, born in 1920) were required to register under a Registration for Employment Order. Many, of course, had already left their homes and volunteered for vital work of one sort or another; the women's Service organisations were building up their strength, there were many thousands of women in civil defence, and by January, 1941, more than nine thousand young women were working on farms or market gardens or in forests as members of the Women's Land Army. The urgent need in the first part of 1941 was for more

Women engaged in munitions work in an East Anglian factory. Engineering works which had in peacetime produced agricultural implements turned to making shells and gun mountings.
Eastern Daily Press

women for the munitions factories. There were a few of these in East Anglia and the *Eastern Daily Press* gave this account of their working life:

> Working 52 hours a week, they earn 45 to 60 shillings a week, including bonus. They are entertained by ENSA concert parties at lunchtime in their canteens. The girls get an excellent lunch for ninepence, also a morning and afternoon cup of tea in the works. They are also able to leave work for two hours on Fridays to do the weekend shopping. The girls are engaged in turning out munitions and equipment.

Most of these young women, at the beginning of 1941, were working near their homes — but most of the war factories were situated in the West and North-west of England or in the Midlands, and so the need was to transfer labour to these areas. By the summer, groups of girls from Norfolk were working in the Midlands factories and the *Eastern Daily Press* reported that, according to one machine-room foreman, they had shown themselves more conscientious than the local girls. As with the men, there were varying reactions to the new compulsion, and many young women did not like the idea of moving to unfamiliar surroundings. Jenny Carr noted the feelings of one Norfolk village girl:

> I asked a girl I know, a clerk in a grocer's office, how old she was and she said: "Oh, don't ask me, I'm so worried. I'm 21 and dreading being uprooted from my job." She said she had decided to do land work, and so had her friend — so that they can stay in the village. She said neither of them were really strong enough, but had made up their minds to try.

In some parts of the Eastern Counties the more conservative farmers had shown a marked lack of enthusiasm for Women's Land Army girls. At a W.L.A. rally in Bury St Edmunds in May it was stated that only 231 women were working on West Suffolk farms and in the county's forests. The farmers had been able to hold to their prejudice because they had been given a government promise that none of their key men would be called up for military service. Agricultural workers were under compulsion to remain at the jobs they were doing, yet even so in 1941 some of them found themselves on the move — to the counties of Leicestershire, Northamptonshire and Warwickshire. In these traditionally grassland counties, where a good

deal of land had been ploughed to grow food, there was a shortage of men with arable experience, and there was a Spring appeal for volunteers to go there. Norfolk, Suffolk and Cambridgeshire men responded.

There was some movement into the region, too. During the early summer the *Eastern Daily Press* published a complaint from a Castle Acre correspondent that Irishmen had been imported to hoe beet in that village. Most were of military age, and they were earning several pounds a week, while Norfolk lads in the Services were getting only a few shillings a week.

In these various ways, very large numbers of men and women and children were constantly on the move, living and working in unfamiliar surroundings, meeting strangers, performing novel new tasks. Britain was moving close, at last, to a complete mobilisation of all its human resources. Apart from bicycles, there was very little personal transport — almost everyone travelled by train or bus, which were invariably packed to capacity. They moved under considerable difficulty, particularly during the blackout, when interior lighting was reduced to a glimmer from blue lamps. Unable to read, people talked more freely. They had more than usual to talk about. Even among pedestrians in the streets one moved after dark through a steady murmur of voices, often of people who could not be seen.

Left: Women took over in the brickfields of the Peterborough area and Bedfordshire as men left for the armed forces. Supplies of bricks were needed for the building of new airfields and for the repair of bomb-damaged buildings.
East Anglian Daily Times

Right: A.T.S. drivers of the 5th London Motor Company, A.T.S., attached to the Royal Army Service Corps at Colchester receiving instruction in engine maintenance and repair.
Imperial War Museum

CHAPTER FIVE

Producing the Food

BEFORE the war Britain had been dependent on large imports of foodstuffs, and home agriculture had been permitted to sink into a state of chronic neglect, nowhere more so than in East Anglia, where dozens of farms had fallen derelict.[1] From the beginning of hostilities, therefore, there had been a drive to increase the area of land under cultivation. The scale of the effort was immense — and the farmers' response was impressive. Under the supervision of War Agricultural Executive Committees, which supplied tractors and labour reinforcements when these were required, over 112,000 additional acres were brought under cultivation in the Eastern Counties in the early months of 1940.

Before the 1940 harvest had even been gathered, the Ministry of Agriculture was discussing with farmers new ploughing quotas for 1941, and by the early weeks of the new year these agreed quotas were being exceeded. In West Suffolk, for example, farmers were asked to plough 13,000 additional acres and had already by 25th January put in hand a greater area than that — some of it land that had not been cultivated since the 1914-18 war. A few weeks later it was announced that Norfolk's quota of 20,000 additional acres had been "exceeded by a considerable margin".

Some of this land was brought back into cultivation only with immense effort and at considerable cost. In Norfolk there were special problems involved with control of water in low-lying areas, as for example the 520 acres of marshes in the Acle district, between Norwich and Great Yarmouth, other large areas of marshland near King's Lynn, and the saltings betwen Wells and Holkham, on the North Norfolk coast, which had been reclaimed from the sea in the nineteenth century. All of these areas were put under the plough. Reclamation proceeded steadily. Potatoes were planted near King's Lynn, wheat and oats elsewhere, sometimes in areas where these crops had not been seen in sixty years.

In Feltwell Fen, further south, the War Agricultural Committee set itself the task of bringing a vast area under cultivation; by the spring of 1941 eight hundred acres had been ploughed and about forty acres a day were being drilled for cereals. At about the same time, about a thousand acres of heath between Saxmundham and Halesworth had been won back and renovated, at a cost of about £15 an acre (the government ploughing grant had been fixed at £2 an acre).

Nothing seemed to be too great a challenge. In April the West Suffolk committee produced a plan to cultivate two thousand acres of Lakenheath Fen, which involved building new roads and bridges. Twenty tractors were set to work; three-quarters of the land was scheduled for potatoes, the other quarter as improved grassland.

Individuals managed prodigious feats, like John Kemp, of Thorpe, who, wrote the *Eastern Daily Press* on 3rd February, "deserved to be held up to the whole country as an example". Although he had a regular job and an allotment of his own, he had volunteered to take over thirteen acres of derelict land owned by Thorpe Parish Council and he had produced 45 tons of sugar beet, a good crop of potatoes, and a small barley crop. Twenty-three land girls working near Norwich produced one million pounds of tomatoes, which were distributed to Midlands towns where tomatoes had virtually disappeared from the shops.

Every acre of land was surveyed — and smaller pieces as well — to check that it was being used to best effect. Every village had its "food production adviser", whose job it was to seek more land, allocate it to whoever would undertake its cultivation, and then give advice and guidance. Common land was taken over. At Cambridge rows of potatoes grew beside the Master's Lodge at St John's. At Bury St Edmunds the Abbey Gardens became one big vegetable plot, growing potatoes, onions, carrots, beans, radishes, lettuces, tomatoes, cabbages and sugar beet, as well as fattening half a dozen pigs with swill collected from premises nearby. In Norwich the City Council agreed that half the municipal golf course should be ploughed, and this example was widely followed — by, among others, the clubs in

Ploughing heathland at Weasenham, between Swaffham and Fakenham, using steam ploughing tackle. The plough is being followed by a caterpillar tractor drawing a rib roller followed by a disc harrow and a heavy harrow. *Eastern Daily Press*

Left: The Minister of Agriculture, Mr R. S. Hudson, drove an engine through sheaves of oats to mark the taking over by his Ministry of the Wissington Light Railway in West Norfolk.
Eastern Daily Press

Right: Mr Hudson took the controls of a tractor while members of the Norfolk War Agricultural Executive Committee rode in the trailer for a tour of inspection of Feltwell Fen.
Eastern Daily Press

Below: Disconsolate golfers look on as one of the fairways at the Norwich municipal golf course is ploughed.
Eastern Daily Press

Mid-Norfolk, at Morley, the l'Estrange Arms at Hunstanton, at Eaton and at Mundesley.

The Ministry of Agriculture gave direction to the county War Agricultural Executive Committees for target production figures. Norfolk, for example, was told to plant 3,500 acres of peas and an additional 3,000 acres of potatoes and 700 acres of onions. At the same time they were given guaranteed prices for these crops: the government would pay £25 a ton for onions, £6 to £9 a ton for carrots, and so on. Some of the decisions taken were experimental, and so involved risks. Rye was planted on poor, light land, for example, on the basis that it could be harvested a fortnight earlier than wheat, which would help to spread the load on the available labour force.

Livestock did not figure large in East Anglian farming at this time. The numbers of sheep fell dramatically. Rationing of livestock fodder was introduced on 1st February, and that was followed by a campaign to increase the amount of silage — Suffolk was given a target production figure of 60,000 tons. At Bressingham sunflowers were grown as a fodder crop. Although machines were being introduced rapidly, there was still a large number of horses on the farms. The Suffolk Horse Society held several very successful sales during the year; one at Ipswich in September attracted such a large entry that it had to be extended to a second day. An interesting sidelight is that the Norwich and District National Master Farriers' and Blacksmiths' Association announced towards the end of the year new prices for shoeing horses: 15s a set for heavy draft horses, 12s a set for farm horses.

Not all farmers measured up to the tasks they were set. By May, 1941, for example, two hundred farmers in Suffolk had been dispossessed of their farms on the grounds that they had shown themselves incapable of cultivating them properly. No other county saw so many of its farmers thrown out — but no other county had seen its farmers before the war reduced to so penurious and demoralised a condition. Some of those whose land was taken over by the War Agricultural Executive Committee blamed tithes for their plight, but there was evidence that Suffolk farmers were generally more conservative in their attitude to new methods than those elsewhere. Normally, dispossession followed only after farmers had had good warning, usually by being taken to court and fined for failure to fulfil ploughing orders.

The government had decided in 1940 that the balance of advantage lay with the adoption of Summer Time (i.e. clocks set one hour in advance of Greenwich Mean Time) on a permanent basis, instead of from April to October. In 1941 it was felt sensible to gain another hour of daylight at the end of the working day by instituting Double Summer Time between 3rd May and 9th August. The farmers were

Members of the Women's Land Army photographed with Lady Denman, Honorary Director of the W.L.A., and county W.L.A. officials at Bury St. Edmunds after they had received badges for eighteen months' work in agriculture. *East Anglian Daily Times*

immediately up in arms; they needed the daylight at the other end of the day. The best they could wring from the government, however, was an understanding that as far as agriculture was concerned its official time would remain unchanged.

One of the main problems of wartime farming was efficient deployment of adequate labour. Key agricultural workers had been given deferment from call-up, and machines were replacing humans on a significant scale (the first combine harvesters arrived in Norfolk in time for the 1940 harvest), but there were serious shortages. The Women's Land Army was designed to fill the gaps and by January, 1941, there were nine thousand land girls at work on farms and smallholdings and in forests throughout England and Wales, and many more being trained at the agricultural colleges and farm institutes and on approved farms. But they were accepted reluctantly on many Eastern Counties farms. The *Eastern Daily Press*, which understood the local mentality only too well, commented editorially in January: "Nothing, we hope, will be said or done in agricultural circles in East Anglia to discourage women from volunteering for land work". At about the same time a spokesmen for the Norfolk W.A.E.C. declared:

> It is certain that farmers will find it necessary to employ more of the Women's Land Army this year. Greater efficiency in farm management, and in the handling of labour in particular, can often produce surprising results.

But eleven months later the Bury St Edmunds branch of the National Farmers' Union placed on record its view that there was too much local prejudice against the W.L.A. girls.

The girls quickly proved themselves highly efficient at almost every task on the farms. They were good with the animals, but they also showed themselves efficient at hedging and ditching, haymaking and harvesting; and they were very much at home, after training, with the new tractors. But there were other, stranger tasks to be learnt. The danger of invasion remained, and there was official anxiety that gas might be used by the enemy. So a drill was prescribed for treatment of farm animals and the W.L.A. girls were often given this responsibility. It involved having ready a stack of damp sacks which could be hung over stable and cowshed windows, chicken coops and kennels, and of materials with which to treat affected animals: a petrol-paraffin mixture with which to wash them down, a solution of bicarbonate of soda with which to bathe their eyes, and an ointment with which to cover any sores caused by the gas which might be used. Fortunately, none ever was, but on many farms there were practice drills.[2]

Steps were also taken to encourage the use of child labour on the farms — a return to a nineteenth-century tradition which had disappeared with the introduction of compulsory full-time education. The Norfolk Education Committee decided in March to advise the managers of its elementary schools to arrange school holidays in accordance with the needs of the farmers for seasonal labour. It insisted that its byelaws relating to the employment of juveniles were in no way being relaxed, but one of its members, Mr E.G. Gooch, who was also president of the

National Union of Agricultural Workers, argued that it was exploitation of children.

There was also a good deal of opposition by members of the West Suffolk County Council to a scheme proposed in May to sponsor children to do harvest work on local farms during the holidays. Later in the year the West Suffolk Education Committee issued summonses against a few parents whose children had taken jobs during school hours. But, at about the same time, Ipswich Education Committee

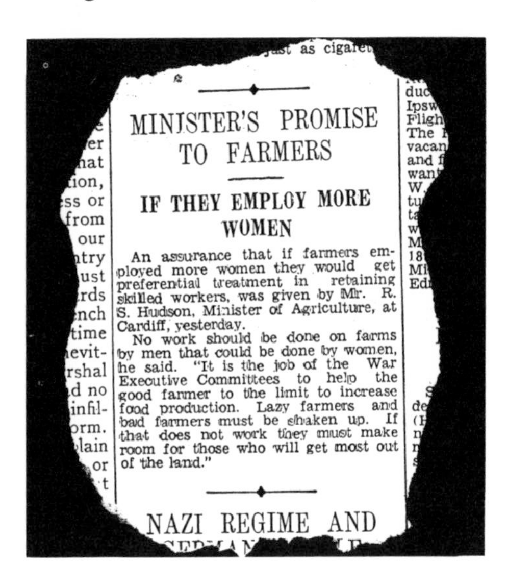

MINISTER'S PROMISE TO FARMERS

IF THEY EMPLOY MORE WOMEN

An assurance that if farmers employed more women they would get preferential treatment in retaining skilled workers, was given by Mr. R. S. Hudson, Minister of Agriculture, at Cardiff, yesterday.

No work should be done on farms by men that could be done by women, he said. "It is the job of the War Executive Committees to help the good farmer to the limit to increase food production. Lazy farmers and bad farmers must be shaken up. If that does not work they must make room for those who will get most out of the land."

NAZI REGIME AND

"No work should be done on farms by men that could be done by women," said the Minister of Agriculture when endeavouring to persuade farmers to accept women on to their farms.
East Anglian Daily Times

gave permission for all children at its junior and senior schools to spend half a day a week picking acorns.

Many schoolchildren did useful work. At King's Lynn, senior boys from King Edward VII School, provided their parents approved, were released from school work for the last five days of term to help with pea picking. Fifty boys from Hackney evacuated to the Freebridge Lynn area also picked peas and potatoes, and other evacuees helped lift sugar beet. Culford School, a public school in Suffolk, incorporated gardening and forestry, and pig, poultry and bee-keeping into its curriculum.

No matter how many young women or part-time children could be recruited to help on the farm, the main burden continued to rest on the shoulders of the regular workers. And they were profoundly dissatisfied with their conditions of employment. At the beginning of 1940 their basic wage had been only thirty-six shillings a week in Suffolk, and a little more in other Eastern Counties. For this they worked forty-eight hours a week in winter and at least fifty in summer. The National Union of Agricultural Workers put in a claim for a £2-a-week minimum, but settled for thirty-eight shillings. Later that year the Ministry of Agriculture introduced a new schedule of farm prices and subsidies and, as part of the package, laid down a minimum weekly wage for all farm workers of forty-eight shillings.

As 1941 opened, the union tabled a new claim for a minimum of £3 a week. The Central Agricultural Wages Board in London met four times in the first half of the year, and adjourned its decision on each occasion. Mr E.G. Gooch, the president of the union and a Norfolk man, warned that the men's patience was nearly exhausted. Another union official said that low morale meant that food production was suffering, and some of the local newspapers published letters from readers expressing support for the men's claim. A Norfolk farmer replied with a letter to the *Eastern Daily Press* published during July:

> How does Mr Gooch think we can pay an increase in wages? With 1½ gallons average per cow, it takes the produce of five cows every week to pay the cowman, who gets 56s.8d. The wholesalers and retailers pay the Milk Marketing Board 1s.8½d. per gallon, and the public pay 2s.8d. and 3s. In May, 1939, maize meal and other feedstuff was £5 a ton; now it is £12 to £14 – when we can get it. We farmers have to take all risks. If milk goes sour in road transport, it comes back. And the loss of cows from disease is terrible, in some years up to a quarter of the herd.

Apart from the Central Wages Board, each county had its own Wages Committee, and that in Norfolk now gave a lead. It resolved at the end of July to

A training class was held at Wickham Market Area School for farmworkers who were having to turn from horses to tractors. Here students are being shown how to remove the transmission gears of a tractor. *East Anglian Daily Times*

After two years of magnificent work, farmers and farmworkers are called upon to grow still more food for man and beast. The Nation's life and health in the coming year may depend upon their efforts—especially those of the next few weeks. In addition to the stubbles, there are nearly two million acres of grassland to be ploughed. Not a moment must be lost. Early ploughing gives better crops.

ISSUED BY THE MINISTRY OF AGRICULTURE AND FISHERIES

Above: Sunflowers were grown as a fodder crop on a farm at Bressingham, in the Waveney Valley near Diss. The seed was fed to poultry, and the stems were used to make paper. *Eastern Daily Press*

Left: "We must strain every nerve to ensure for ourselves still further production at home," says the Minister of Agriculture in this advertisement issued by his Ministry. *East Anglian Daily Times*

Right: It was not only those women who joined the W.L.A. who worked on the farms. These residents of Playford were lifting and topping sugar beet, well wrapped up against the December cold. *East Anglian Daily Times*

give adult male farm workers an additional six shillings a week, which was half of what the men had been seeking. This established a new minimum of fifty-four shillings, and Essex and Hertfordshire quickly followed suit. The Cambridgeshire Committee did better, agreeing a fifty-five shillings minimum, but the Suffolk farmers continued doggedly to resist any increase. Eventually, in mid-October, they fell into line and paid fifty-four shillings, but not before the *Bury Free Press* had published critical editorial comment, arguing that it was "manifestly unfair that Suffolk should remain on the lowest level for an indefinite period, while other men have received increases."

No sooner had this situation been reached, however, than the Cambridgeshire committee reconsidered the matter and passed a resolution in favour of the full £3 a week that had been claimed. This went to a meeting of the Central Agricultural Wages Board in November, and it agreed unanimously to fix the national minimum at £3 as from the end of the year. The Cambridgeshire committee then agreed a scale of payments for special categories of workers, so that cowmen, horsemen and shepherds were assured of at least £3 10s. a week. As the year ended, the Suffolk farmers were still protesting their inability to pay £3.

Despite these difficulties, it was generally agreed that farmers and farm workers between them had done a good job during 1941. Norfolk alone had grown about a quarter of the British sugarbeet crop. It had brought more than 750,000 acres under the plough, so that the proportion of available land in the county under arable cultivation was as great as it had been in 1870-90, when Norfolk arable farming had been in its heyday. Norfolk fruitgrowers suffered because of unfavourable Spring weather but still did well. More than a third of the total blackcurrant crop produced by members of Norfolk Fruit Growers Ltd was requisitioned by the government for its scheme for issuing fruit juice to children.

Even before the 1941 harvest was dealt with, Whitehall had sent forth its instructions for 1942 planting. Norfolk, as an example, was told it must have a minimum of 105,000 acres of wheat, 92,500 acres of sugar beet, 35,000 acres of potatoes, and so on. Each county similarly received its orders, and it was the responsibility of the Agricultural Executive Committees to see that they were obeyed.

To supplement these tremendous efforts in 1941 by the agricultural industry, the government launched a new "Dig for Victory" campaign to encourage individuals to get busy in their gardens and to rent and cultivate allotments, A colour film, *The Garden Goes to War*, was widely shown; it explained how to prepare the soil, sow and plant, harvest and store, and how to deal with pests and diseases. Competitions were organised, leaflets issued and lectures given, and village "food production clubs" set up.

Every village, it was suggested, should grow all the vegetables it needed to see it through the whole year, and so the emphasis should be on non-perishables. The Women's Institutes played a big part in this campaign; women were urged to do a few hours' gardening each week, and they received a great deal of advice on food preservation. At Cambridge the "Food Advice Centre" had seven hundred callers a week, many of them wanting information about preserving, bottling and jam-making; many men who had grown food on their allotments wanted to make sure it was used in the best way. At Thetford a dozen evacuee mothers took over half an acre of neglected allotment, took instruction from a local Women's Voluntary Service official, and in a few weeks had it double-trenched and planted with potatoes, beans and marrows. Employers were urged to make any vacant land beside their factories available to their employees to grow food.

The result of all these efforts did not meet Britain's food requirements. It was essential to continue to import large quantities from overseas. After May, 1941, a considerable proportion of these imports came across the Atlantic as part of the United States' "Lend-Lease" supplies. The first such consignment was received by the Minister of Food with great ceremony — four million eggs, 120,000 pounds of cheese and one thousand tons of flour. Despite the German efforts at blockade, the government was just able to ensure the minimum amount of food required to keep the nation healthy. But it proved almost as difficult a task to share it out fairly as it was to get it into the storehouses.

CHAPTER SIX

Fair Shares All Round

STANDING with their backs to the wall and facing tremendous odds, the British people insisted on one basic principle: so far as was possible, the cost and the effort of national defence, the hardship and sacrifice involved, must be equally shared by *everyone*. Official propaganda presented a picture of a classless society, united in conviction and will — "we're all in this together". The organisation and discipline required to secure maximum effort, production and fighting strength did not allow for much individual enterprise or initiative. What was wanted was an effective war machine, and individuals were cogs in that machine.

As shortages of food and other basic requirements became more acute during the course of 1941, there were a few individuals, the irrepressible entrepreneurs, who could not resist the temptation to make money for themselves by exploiting the laws of supply and demand. Thus was born a "black market" in ration coupons and in those items in especially short supply, operated by a breed of shady characters who were called "spivs". Of course, their activities were illegal, but much of the public chose to ridicule rather than revile then. Comedians shuffled up to their stooges on stage and inquired, from the corner of their mouths: "Wanna 'nother pound of sugar?" This tolerance suggested that a good many people may have enjoyed a little extra over and above the ration from time to time. But it does not change the fact that without an official policy of — and popular belief in — egalitarianism, Britain's will to survive would have been seriously undermined.

Rationing was designed to ensure that everyone — the rich man and woman in their castle and the poor couple near their gate — received no more than their fair share of the available food and clothing and fuel. The slogan favoured by the Minister of Food, Lord Woolton, was "Fair shares all round".

As 1941 began, there had been a full year's experience of rationing, for sugar, bacon and butter had been rationed since November, 1939. All other meat had been rationed since March, 1940, there having been a few months' delay while a control system was created under which the Ministry of Food purchased all meat and livestock from the producers. Meat was rationed by price; adults were entitled to 1s.2d. worth each week, children to seven pennyworth. The butchers grumbled more than the customers; they held a meeting at Bury St Edmunds and declared that their profits had been reduced to nothing. A few months later the rations were reduced, sugar from twelve to eight ounces per person per week and butter from eight to four ounces. But perhaps the greatest hardship was felt when rationing of tea to two ounces a week began in July, 1941.

Country folk had a clear advantage over those in the towns, because they were able to produce by their own efforts — and a little sensible barter — most of the food they needed. When a Mass Observation representative visited Alderton, near Woodbridge, in May, he called at the village shop to buy something for his supper, but could get only a tin of sardines and a tin of peas. There were no other canned foods, no bread, and no fruit, chocolate or cigarettes when he called at 5 p.m. But when he had had a little time to acclimatise, he noted that there was very little talk about food shortages. He deduced that there must be a good supply of garden produce, and when he called at a local farm the lady of the house told him, cheerfully: "We go short for nothing, and we don't intend to. There's cream in the dairy, and fowls and pigs in the yard. We couldn't live on what the rations allow."(1)

Up in Norfolk, Bunty Carr noted in her diary during June:

> We had one of our hens for lunch, with our own new potatoes and carrots, but we felt very guilty about it.

Rabbit was rediscovered as a succulent dish, and clubs were set up to encourage small-scale breeding. In January wood pigeons were selling in London at 1s.10d., which was nearly four times their price a year earlier. The Food Ministry urged

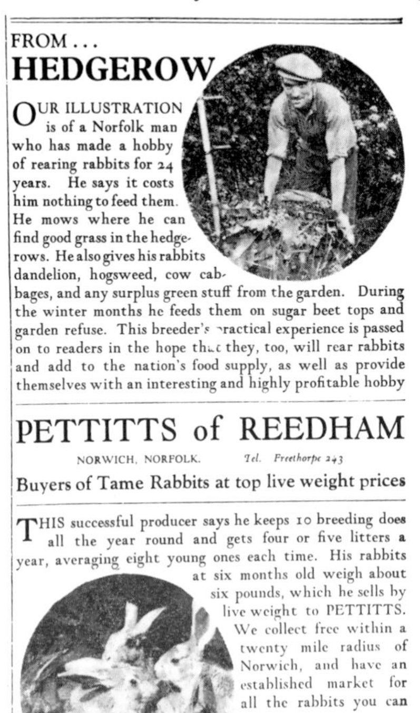

Rabbits were an important source of food in wartime Britain, as this advertisement indicates.
Eastern Daily Press

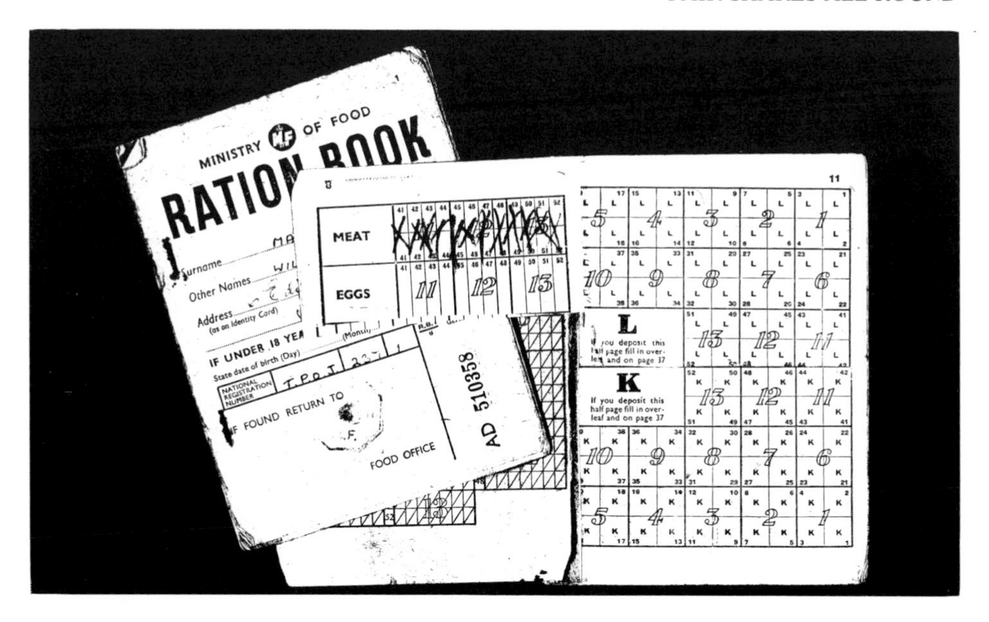

people to gather blackberries and rose-hips from the hedgerows, the latter because they could be made into a syrup with a high vitamin C content. During September most East Anglian lanes saw picking parties almost every day. Thirty children from Stratford St Mary council school, for example, collected 840lb of blackberries, sold them to a local jam factory, and bought twelve pullets for egg production.

As we have already noted, meat, sugar and butter had long been rationed, and tea was rationed from July, 1941. For these foods, each individual held a ration book and surrendered the appropriate number of coupons from it week by week, as the food was purchased. But there were other ways of trying to distribute food fairly than by fixing individual rations. Traders had to register, and received bulk allocations of certain goods in line with the number of customers they supplied. Mrs Sarah Williams, who was employed at the Ministry of Food office in Sheringham, wrote in her diary during the summer:

> . . . piles and piles of instructions about slaughtering of pigs, registration of establishments for milk and eggs. We sent out jam and syrup permits to bakers today, wrote more harvest permits, did a few annual feeding-stuff permits, and took phone calls, largely from milk retailers informing us they wouldn't retail milk under the rationing scheme. All this milk business is made difficult because we have also the Milk Marketing Board to cope with. The poor farmers feel quite confused, having separate sets of instructions to cope with.

As 1941 began the Ministry of Food had urged the public to "Drink More Milk", and the response had been good. But by April milk supplies were falling off, and it was decreed that the public should receive fifteen per cent less. The retailers were left with the responsibility of securing this reduction. In Norwich most of them agreed that they should stop delivering on one day a week, but after trying this on two successive Thursdays they hurriedly changed their minds, so great was the outcry. Similarly in Bury St Edmunds roundsmen and women reported widespread insults from their customers, and the local food office was beseiged with requests for additional milk. In Cambridge, too, an attempt to cut out one daily delivery brought widespread protests. The trouble rumbled on for the rest of the year, the

LEMONS

We are expecting a considerable consignment of Murcia Lemons within the next few days. We shall be pleased to receive orders from Fruiterers and Grocers, and allotments made will as far as possible comply with same.

(Retail controlled price 6½d. lb.)

E. PORDAGE & CO., LTD.
NORWICH

C. ROWLAND & SON, LTD.
GT. YARMOUTH

Lemons were very scarce and those consignments which did reach the ports were distributed and sold under strict controls.
Eastern Daily Press

government seeking to improve the system of registration and hinting that a stricter rationing system might have to be introduced, some dairies instituting their own rationing scheme and letting no-one have more than a pint of milk per person per day. As the year ended, the problem had not been resolved and the *Bury Free Press* published a strong editorial criticism of what it saw as official muddle. Almost as much milk was being produced as in peacetime, it argued, but demand had increased. It called for a fairer distribution, after guarantees of adequate supplies to children, expectant mothers and invalids.

As the months passed, more and more important items of diet became difficult to find. In February a "national wholemeal loaf" was introduced, using 85 per cent extraction flour, and it was sometimes difficult to buy white bread. Distribution was uneven. By December bread was in short supply in some areas: in Ipswich and

King's Lynn bakers cancelled their deliveries on one day a week. Yet when John Rogers took a trip from Ipswich to Felixstowe, he noted:

> When I arrived there at 3.20 p.m. I was amazed at the amount of cakes in the shops — these are "an event" in Ipswich. There were plenty of chocolates, too; I bought a welcome pound of them.

Sarah Williams decided to travel out of Sheringham to try her luck as a housewife and she reported a similar experience:

> I went to Holt and managed to buy some Puffed Wheat, a tin of salmon, some tomatoes, and some soap flakes, which was a satisfactory thing to have achieved, none of these being obtainable at the moment in Sheringham.

A fortnight earlier this same diarist noted:

> There is great excitement among the housewives in the town, because one shop has some lemons for sale. I remember, a day or two ago, eating bread and cheese and onions with a feeling of triumph and luxury!

Oranges and lemons were particularly prized; searching for them became something of a treasure hunt. A consignment of South African oranges which arrived in June was directed to the heavily-bombed Great Yarmouth and Gorleston area. After a priority distribution to local hospitals and doctors' patients, the remainder were sold in Yarmouth market at sixpence a pound. The next shipment, of about one million oranges, was more widely distributed; the Ipswich and Saxmundham areas received 1,900 cases, and Lowestoft, Bury St Edmunds and parts of Norfolk received a share. Sometimes news of shipments preceded the actual arrival of the fruit, and everyone was on tenterhooks. Attempts to profiteer were firmly dealt with, as when a Fakenham woman was fined £10 for selling four lemons at a price above the 6½d. a pound permitted maximum.

Shortages of eggs, sugar, and tobacco and cigarettes seem to have caused the public real dismay. Cecil Sparks, a special constable living near Norwich, wrote plaintively in his diary:

> Only three eggs each for August. How is one to feed a young baby properly when his diet should include one egg per day? Fortunately, we live near a small poultry farm, where we are able to get an occasional extra.

Sarah Williams described in her diary a typical day at the Food Office:

> . . . a very busy day again. The country buses came in today, bringing in all the farm labourers' wives who want extra cheese for their husbands and sons. They find it difficult to feed their families on the present rations, particularly now that eggs are scarcer . . . But it is very rare to hear any real complaining.

Cheese had been in short supply for several months. The Ministry of Food instructed caterers not to serve more than one-twentieth of an ounce with any meal — and none at all if the meal included meat.

Extra sugar was made available to Women's Institutes for jam making (the East Suffolk Institutes alone made twenty-nine tons of it), but individual housewives thought they deserved some extra as well. They did not get it until October, when the ration was increased from eight to twelve ounces. At that same time the ration of fats went up from eight to ten ounces, and canteens were promised that they would receive more meat. The increases were said to have been made "to help the public through the winter".

From 1st December, however, tinned meats, fish and vegetables were brought under a points rationing system. With their sixteen points per person per month allocation, customers could buy whatever they fancied — if they could find it! A tin of salmon could take a whole month's coupons.

By the Autumn of 1941 the food situation had become critical, and some things came to the shops irregularly. Price control was imposed on chocolate and sweets in September; dried fruit, although not officially rationed, was distributed on the basis of twelve ounces per month per person. There were complaints in some areas that butter on sale was stale or rancid; the *Cambridge Daily News* offered its readers the advice: "Stand in cold water with a pinch of bicarb for two hours." Cambridge butchers managed to maintain their annual dinner, and announced that they "did their best to feed the public — not to satisfy them", adding darkly that "some of them are impossible to satisfy".

The Ministry of Food called for the setting up of Kitchen Clubs to provide information and give demonstrations of gas and electric cooking. It placed regular advertisements in the local newspapers offering new recipes: highly inventive dishes such as "carrot hotpot". Some food firms also offered imaginative ideas; a manufacturer of processed cheese, which was not at that stage rationed, suggested "cheese chops" and "cheese casserole".

As to tobacco, the problem is best illustrated by this extract from Bunty Carr's diary, describing what happened at her small village store:

> We received a small consignment of tobacco and cigarettes and at 4.30 p.m. all the old men in the village were practically running down the road. I only had eight ounces of tobacco between thirty of them. Those who got some did not take kindly to my suggestion that they should divide it up. We were harassed all the evening by men and boys after cigarettes.

Later on, Bunty Carr's sense of morality seems to have been bruised by her experiences, for in August she confessed to her diary:

> I had a nice sized mill cheese for a present, with the inquiry "Had we any tobacco?" Decided to start bartering tobacco for food.

Mass Observation interviewed another person with a confused sense of propriety. He had travelled from Ipswich to Felixstowe because he had heard that there was a lot of tobacco on sale there. But then he complained:

> As usual, the Ipswich people spoilt it, coming down with despatch cases and so on.[2]

There was plenty of good advice available in wartime Britain, including recipes issued by the Ministry of Food for making use of potatoes.
East Anglian Daily Times

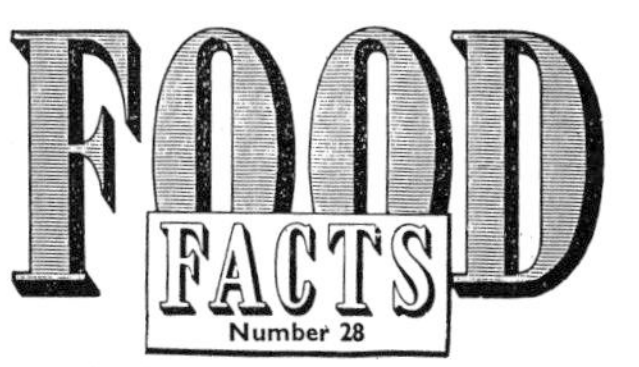

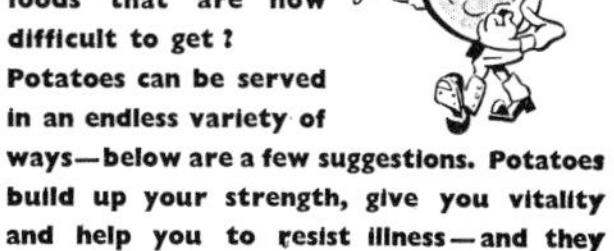

HAVE you discovered how often potatoes can replace foods that are now difficult to get? Potatoes can be served in an endless variety of ways—below are a few suggestions. Potatoes build up your strength, give you vitality and help you to resist illness—and they are home-grown. So eat them often.

ON THE KITCHEN FRONT

Wartime "Champ"

Here is a wartime version of the old Irish dish, Champ. Scrub and slice 1 lb. potatoes and 1 lb. carrots. Put in a saucepan with a teacupful of hot salted water and add a small cabbage finely shredded. Cover with the lid, cook steadily, giving an occasional shake until tender (about 15 minutes). The water should have just boiled away by then. Add a small teacupful of hot milk and mash well with a dash of pepper and more salt if necessary. Serve at once with a pat of margarine to each helping.

Our sailors don't mind risking their lives to feed you and your family—but they do mind if you help the U-boats by wasting food.

Save those Orange Rinds!

Here's a new way to make use of orange peel. Grate it and mix a little with mashed potatoes. The potatoes will turn an exciting pink colour.

Potato Pastry

This is extremely good with either sweet or savoury dishes. Sieve 8 ozs. plain flour with ¼ teaspoonful salt. Rub in 4 ozs. cooking fat with the tips of the fingers, until the mixture has the appearance of fine bread-crumbs. Add 4 ozs. sieved cooked potato and rub lightly into the other ingredients. Mix to a very dry dough with a little cold water. Knead well with the fingers and roll out.

Hot Potato Salad

Cook some potatoes in their skins, and when just done, peel and cut them in slices. Have ready mixed a dressing of pepper, salt, a little sugar, oil, vinegar, mustard and hot milk. Mix the potatoes thoroughly with the dressing and add some chopped parsley, or, if you have any, a little chopped onion. Serve hot.

Experiment with your meals as much as you can. It gives variety and it does you good.

Potato Suet Crust

This recipe will make your suet ration go further and give you a light crust, which is not greasy. Mix 8 ozs. flour, 2 ozs. suet, 2 ozs. grated raw potato, salt and a little water. Then cook your mixture in the usual way.

Ambrose Heath is this week's speaker on the Radio Kitchen Front at 8.15 every morning.

THE MINISTRY OF FOOD, LONDON, S.W.1

The same Mass Observation report on Ipswich, in September, noted queues for cigarettes, bread and sweets, and added:

> For some time there has been a rumour in the town that, because this is an evacuation area, people are deliberately being kept short of food, so that there should be no over-crowding. But there does not seem to be any more of a shortage in Ipswich than in other places.(2)

The queue was a regular feature of most towns in this region. The *Lynn Advertiser* discussed this phenomenon in a leading article on 13th June:

> Lynn and West Norfolk traders are still, for the most part, managing to avoid that wartime bogey, the queue. Pork butchers are not always able to prevent a gathering of customers outside their premises on the morning when they open, but by dint of having sausages, etc. weighed up in advance, and persuading people to tender the exact amount of cash, such queues are fairly quickly dispersed.

This newspaper was not alone in trying to dissuade the public from queuing; the *Bury Free Press* also deprecated this behaviour and warned that the local police were considering a prohibition of queues. Very sensibly, the authorities had second thoughts; the fact was that many people formed a habit of queuing and looked forward to meeting their friends and gossiping there.

People were sometimes prosecuted for wasting food. In February the assistant Master of the Downham Market Institution was fined £5 and ordered to pay costs when he was found guilty of wasting 10lb 10oz of bread, valued at 1s. 4d., and in July a Cambridge woman whose baker left more bread than she needed and who threw fourteen pounds of it into the garden for the birds was fined.

The local courts were kept busy with prosecutions of those who broke the rationing or price control regulations. The range of possible offences is indicated by these few examples, taken at random from the newspapers of the time:

March: Downham magistrates fined a man 9s. because he used coupons from his wife's ration book, though she was not living with him at the time.
A Norfolk butcher and four of his customers were fined because he supplied each of them with 5½d. worth of meat in excess of their rations.

May: A Cambridge market stallholder was summoned for overcharging for poultry.

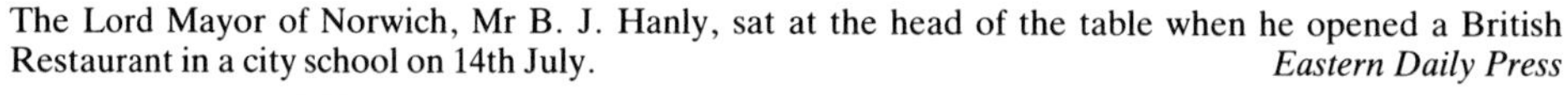

The Lord Mayor of Norwich, Mr B. J. Hanly, sat at the head of the table when he opened a British Restaurant in a city school on 14th July. *Eastern Daily Press*

June: A Norfolk butcher's manager was sent to prison for nine months for receiving meat stolen from an R.A.F. station where, according to the prosecution, there had been "terrible laxity".

August: A Buxton butcher was fined £20 for slaughtering two cows without a Ministry of Food licence.
Several people were fined at Bury St Edmunds for selling eggs when they were not licensed to do so.

November: The makers and the sellers of a "lemon substitute" were prosecuted at Cambridge because it contained no citric acid or vitamin C.

It was still possible to eat away from home in restaurants and canteens, but ration coupons had to be surrendered. Early in 1941 the government decided that communal feeding centres might help the situation. As soon as he was informed of the proposal, Winston Churchill sent a memorandum to the Minister of Food:

> I hope the term "communal feeding centres" is not going to be adopted. It is an odious expression, suggestive of Communism and the workhouse. I suggest you call them "British Restaurants". Everybody associates the word "restaurant" with a good meal, and they may as well have the name, if they cannot get anything else.(3)

Churchill did not act quickly enough to prevent the first ones being opened as "communal feeding centres", but by mid-year they were British Restaurants. Ipswich, first off the mark, opened one in January, and there was one in Dereham at about the same time. A blunt appraisal of service at the Ipswich centre, after it had had a few months to settle down, is provided by an entry in the diary of a local man:

> Had lunch at our Communal Feeding Centre, and did not get too bad a meal. Stood in a queue for tickets and got ten pennyworth: two at 1d., one at 6d., and one at 2d. Parting with the penny token, I was given a plate of soup and a piece of bread — not too bad, but a bit too much pearl barley in the soup. In exchange for my sixpenny ticket, I got cold roast beef, salad and potatoes — quite good, but I could have done with a bit more of it. For the twopenny ticket, I got a piece of date pudding . . . The odd penny went on a cup of tea. The Centre was quite full. It was clean, and there were quite a few good-class people there. We sat on our own, at a table to hold eight. The menu was chalked up outside, and notices told us not to waste food, as it is a munition of war. I may go there again.

Diss opened a Centre in March and, in the first two weeks, it served 2,427 meals. By June Swaffham was so impressed by the reports it had heard from Dereham that it was taking steps to follow suit. Great Yarmouth opened one in mid-July, housed in the Hospital School, and, like the others, staffed by W.V.S. volunteers; but this was at first announced as an experiment and catered only for civil defence workers. It opened each day, served meals free to on-duty civil defence personnel, and, if they came there when they were off duty, charged them eightpence for a meal which, typically, might consist of roast beef, batter pudding and vegetables, followed by gooseberries and custard. When Norwich opened a British Restaurant at the Bull Close School in July, it provided music for dancing in an adjoining room. Later in the year it opened two more. By the end of the year most towns had them, and they were well patronised. Dereham reported on its first year's operation that 50,846 dinners had been served at sevenpence a head for adults, fivepence a head for children aged five to fourteen, and threepence a head for infants. The only paid staff had been a cook and one helper; the rest of the work had been done by the W.V.S. There was expected to be a profit of £160. There

Not the staff of a British Restaurant but members of the W.V.S. giving a demonstration of open-air emergency cooking in New Square, Cambridge. Lunches cooked in an oven made of bricks were sold to the public at sixpence a meal.
Cambridge Daily News

were proposals towards the end of the year to provide a mobile "cash-and-carry" service to some villages.

By this time, too, most schools were able to supply hot midday meals to their pupils; in Norfolk they cost fourpence. Bunty Carr attended a Workers' Educational Association one-day class at a new school in King's Lynn during June and afterwards wrote in her diary:

> I was amused to find that a good proportion of the people had gone because of the excellent teas served in the school canteen, which apparently always start with hot meat patties.

Closely linked with food supply was the question of health. The unfamiliar surroundings in which many people found themselves, the separation of children from their families, the frequent crowding together in public shelters, the loss of sleep, all of these things brought new health hazards. In the early months of 1941 the emphasis was on immunisation against diptheria. This had been available free to all children for years past, but many had not had it done; now a brisk propaganda campaign produced excellent results. In Newmarket, Haverhill and Hadleigh, for example, it was announced that a hundred per cent of children had been immunised. After a special appeal by the Mayor of Bury St Edmunds, 2,274 pupils in elementary schools in the town queued up for a jab. By April over 13,000 schoolchildren in East Suffolk had been treated.

The campaign was considered to have been a great success. The annual report of the School Medical Officer for the City and County of Norwich summed up:

> 1941 was a comparatively successful year, in spite of the war . . . With the exception of a very small rise in diphtheria, and some activity in whooping cough, the infectious diseases were less than in 1940.

There had, in fact, been fifty-one cases of diphtheria during the year, with four deaths, and 361 cases of whooping cough, with five deaths. The County Medical

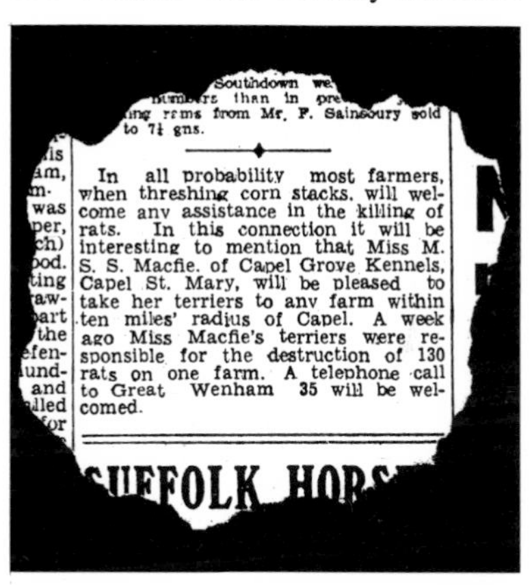

Southdown we
...than in pre...
...ing rams from Mr. F. Sainsbury sold to 7½ gns.

In all probability most farmers, when threshing corn stacks, will welcome any assistance in the killing of rats. In this connection it will be interesting to mention that Miss M. S. S. Macfie, of Capel Grove Kennels, Capel St. Mary, will be pleased to take her terriers to any farm within ten miles' radius of Capel. A week ago Miss Macfie's terriers were responsible for the destruction of 130 rats on one farm. A telephone call to Great Wenham 35 will be welcomed.

SUFFOLK HORS...

Vermin not merely ate valuable food supplies but posed a health hazard, and various means were employed to reduce the numbers of rats.
East Anglian Daily Times

Officer of Health, reporting on the county as a whole, revealed that there had been 158 deaths from pneumonia, 149 from tuberculosis, thirteen from whooping cough, nine from diphtheria, seven from measles, and twenty-three from other infectious diseases. There were some restrictions on what was possible. In some places doctors had gone into the Services — at Loddon, for example, the parish council was concerned when in March there were two hundred children waiting for immunisation and no doctor. When Sarah Williams went to have her eyes tested at Sheringham, she found:

> There were only two sorts of frames to choose from — more war-time restrictions.

There was constant harping on the need for cleanliness. It was widely believed that many of the London evacuees had brought fleas, bugs and lice with them. There was a plague of rats; when the East Suffolk War Agricultural Committee organised a campaign during February and March no fewer than 59,734 rat carcases were produced for payment of a reward. Up to the autumn of 1941 professional ratcatchers and gamekeepers mainly employed on destruction of vermin were not called up unless they were under thirty.

There seemed to be many more mice, too, which was attributed to people having got rid of their cats because of the air raids. Pets often had a hard time. Cambridgeshire War Agricultural Committee was told at the end of the year that abandoned dogs had attached themselves to military units, had followed them when they moved, and had then caused a great deal of trouble among in-lamb flocks in the west of the county.

Food was, of course, only one of the things that was rationed. From the outbreak of the war, supplies of the "pool" petrol — a standard medium-octane blend sold at 1s. 6d. a gallon — were issued to private motorists in relation to the horsepower of their vehicles; four gallons a month for the smallest cars, ten gallons

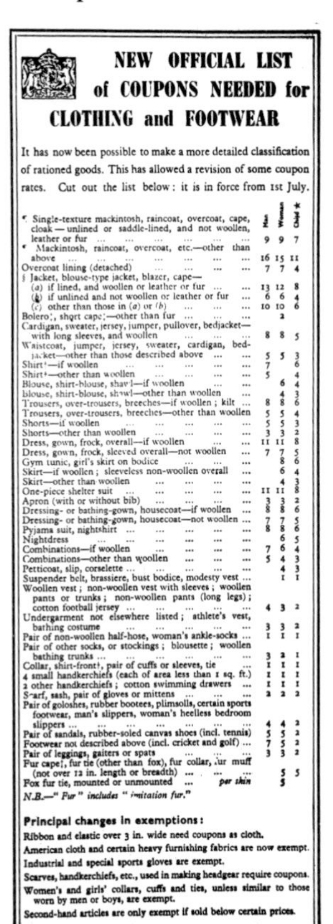

NEW OFFICIAL LIST of COUPONS NEEDED for CLOTHING and FOOTWEAR

It has now been possible to make a more detailed classification of rationed goods. This has allowed a revision of some coupon rates. Cut out the list below: it is in force from 1st July.

	Man	Woman	Child ★
* Single-texture mackintosh, raincoat, overcoat, cape, cloak — unlined or saddle-lined, and not woollen, leather or fur ...	9	9	7
* Mackintosh, raincoat, overcoat, etc.—other than above ...	16	15	11
Overcoat lining (detached) ...	7	7	4
¶ Jacket, blouse-type jacket, blazer, cape— (a) if lined, and woollen or leather or fur ...	13	12	8
(b) if unlined and not woollen or leather or fur ...	6	6	4
(c) other than those in (a) or (b) ...	10	10	6
Bolero‡, short cape‡—other than fur ...		2	
Cardigan, sweater, jersey, jumper, pullover, bedjacket—with long sleeves, and woollen ...	8	8	5
Waistcoat, jumper, jersey, sweater, cardigan, bedjacket—other than those described above ...	5	5	3
Shirt†—if woollen ...	7		6
Shirt†—other than woollen ...	5		4
Blouse, shirt-blouse, shawl—if woollen ...		6	4
Blouse, shirt-blouse, shawl—other than woollen ...		4	3
Trousers, over-trousers, breeches—if woollen; kilt ...	8	8	6
Trousers, over-trousers, breeches—other than woollen	5	5	4
Shorts—if woollen ...	5	5	3
Shorts—other than woollen ...	3	3	2
Dress, gown, frock, overall—if woollen ...	11	11	8
Dress, gown, frock, sleeved overall—not woollen ...	7	7	5
Gym tunic, girl's skirt on bodice ...		8	6
Skirt—if woollen; sleeveless non-woollen overall ...		6	4
Skirt—other than woollen ...		4	3
One-piece shelter suit ...	11	11	8
Apron (with or without bib) ...	3	3	2
Dressing- or bathing-gown, housecoat—if woollen ...	8	8	6
Dressing- or bathing-gown, housecoat—not woollen ...	7	7	5
Pyjama suit, nightshirt ...	8	8	6
Nightdress ...		6	5
Combinations—if woollen ...	7	6	4
Combinations—other than woollen ...	5	4	3
Petticoat, slip, corselette ...		4	3
Suspender belt, brassiere, bust bodice, modesty vest ...		1	1
Woollen vest; non-woollen vest with sleeves; woollen pants or trunks; non-woollen pants (long legs); cotton football jersey ...	4	3	2
Undergarment not elsewhere listed; athlete's vest, bathing costume ...	3	3	2
Pair of non-woollen half-hose, woman's ankle-socks ...	1	1	1
Pair of other socks, or stockings; blousette; woollen bathing trunks ...	3	2	1
Collar, shirt-front†, pair of cuffs or sleeves, tie ...	1	1	1
4 small handkerchiefs (each of area less than 1 sq. ft.)	1	1	1
2 other handkerchiefs; cotton swimming drawers ...	1	1	1
Scarf, sash, pair of gloves or mittens ...	2	2	2
Pair of goloshes, rubber bootees, plimsolls, certain sports footwear, man's slippers, woman's heelless bedroom slippers ...	4	4	2
Pair of sandals, rubber-soled canvas shoes (incl. tennis)	5	5	2
Footwear not described above (incl. cricket and golf) ...	7	5	2
Pair of leggings, gaiters or spats ...	3	3	2
Fur cape‡, fur tie (other than fox), fur collar, fur muff (not over 12 in. length or breadth) ...		5	5
Fox fur tie, mounted or unmounted ... *per skin*		5	

N.B.—"Fur" includes "imitation fur."

Principal changes in exemptions:

Ribbon and elastic over 3 in. wide need coupons as cloth.

American cloth and certain heavy furnishing fabrics are now exempt.

Industrial and special sports gloves are exempt.

Scarves, handkerchiefs, etc., used in making headgear require coupons.

Women's and girls' collars, cuffs and ties, unless similar to those worn by men or boys, are exempt.

Second-hand articles are only exempt if sold below certain prices.

* Sizes exempt from Purchase Tax † With or without collar attached. ¶ For women's garments over 28 in. long. ‡ For women's garments over 16 in. but not over 28 in. long. ‡ Not over 16 inches long.

ISSUED BY THE BOARD OF TRADE

Clothing was rationed from 1st June, but those on war work who had to buy their own uniforms could get them without giving up "coupons". *Eastern Daily Press*

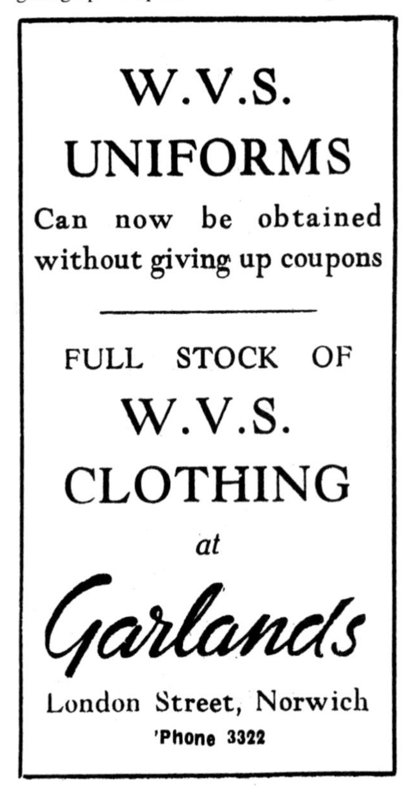

for the largest. "Supplementary" coupons were issued to those who proved a valid business reason. Commercial vehicles were issued with petrol which had been dyed red, to discourage its misuse.

Every drop of petrol had to be imported, with seamen's lives at risk, and from time to time protests were heard at the way some of the petrol was used. A popular wartime film which featured the lives of a transatlantic tanker crew contained the line: "That ought to be enough to take quite a few racegoers to Newmarket". During July race traffic congestion there brought critical comment in the House of Commons. The *Eastern Daily Press* published a letter in April which complained that too many people were using their cars to drive to dinner parties. Bunty Carr noted in her diary:

> Two commercial travellers from rival firms in Norwich came in the same car, to save petrol. Neither of them appeared to be able to supply anything I wanted.

There were regular prosecutions of those who "fiddled" petrol; as an example, a Norwich girl van driver had to pay a £2 fine and £6 costs when she was found guilty of unlawfully possessing three supplementary petrol coupons. The basic petrol ration was maintained throughout 1941, but a twenty per cent reduction in paraffin supplies during the summer caused problems in rural areas, where many people depended on paraffin for heating, lighting and cooking. Candles were in short supply, and several local authorities made urgent representations to the Petroleum Board in London as the winter set in.

To save petrol, a Norwich solicitor, Mr Ronald Keefe, travelled to Wymondham Petty Sessions in a pony and trap, and there were many others in the region who happily reverted to an earlier form of transport.

For a time it was possible to circumvent the strict rationing system by hiring a car. Cecil Sparks, noting a respite from his duties as special constable, wrote in his diary in October:

> I hired a "drive yourself" car for two days, just to enable my wife to get out with the baby. I felt that was a justifiable use of a gallon or so of petrol (we didn't do above 50 miles), especially as she had had no holiday. But I was surprised to find that there was petrol available for such purposes. Today I have come across another use to which these cars are being put. A traveller, unable to do all his journeys on the petrol allotted him for his own car, hires one of these "drive yourself" cars for a fortnight . . . Of course, he has to pay dearly for the use, but nevertheless something seems to be wrong somewhere. It is certainly an example of one law for the rich and another for the poor . . .

Within a month after this entry the government brought in a new restriction to prevent this abuse.

Clothing and footwear were rationed from 1st June, 1941. Each person was given sixty-six coupons for the first year; an unlined raincoat for a man required the surrender of nine coupons, a jacket thirteen, a pair of socks three, a pair of shoes seven; women had to surrender eleven coupons for a dress, seven for a skirt, six for a nightgown, five for a pair of shoes. The most striking effect was seen in the wedding photographs in the newspapers; many brides still managed to get married in white, but short dresses were commonplace, and some brides wore suits at their weddings. As late as November, however, fur coats were still on sale and assurances were offered that artificial silk stockings would continue to be available. They usually took a lot of finding!

The government introduced a newsprint rationing scheme early in the year and the number of pages in the local newspapers was drastically reduced — the *Cambridge Daily News*, for example, contained only eight pages. Prices went up, too, from a penny to three-halfpence.

During the course of the year, virtually everything was in short supply at some time or other, quite apart from the goods officially rationed. In June it was announced that public houses in Bury St Edmunds would close on Wednesday and Saturday afternoons, because of restricted supplies, and Newmarket pubs ran out of beer completely in July. Ipswich publicans and hoteliers announced that from 23rd August they would open from 11 a.m. to 1.30 p.m. and from 5.30 to 10 p.m., "supplies permitting".

Coal was also sometimes in short supply. There were complaints during August that some Cambridgeshire villagers could only get it if they went to the railway station and transported it themselves. In June guidance was offered from Whitehall to rural authorities in Norfolk to collect and store all old timber, as it might be needed as a substitute for coal during the coming winter.

Women were even employed on navvying jobs and were employed on the building of new airfields in East Anglia. Here they are laying drainage pipes alongside the concrete runway. *Eastern Daily Press*

CHAPTER SEVEN

Change of Fortune

THE MOOD of the British people changed at midsummer. Until then it had been characterised by a dogged "We can take it" attitude. This was brutal realism; "take it" was all they could do, at that stage, when survival was the basic purpose and defeat of the enemy a distant prospect. During the second half of the year conditions on the home front did not change significantly; indeed, in some respects they became more difficult. What was transformed was the balance of power between the Allied and the Axis powers.

On 22nd June Hitler's armies invaded Soviet Russia, the main weight of the German war effort was swung eastward and Britain no longer stood alone. By that time, too, there had been important developments in Anglo-American relations.

Prime Minister Winston Churchill had never doubted that victory depended upon the participation of the United States, and in the first weeks of 1941 Roosevelt's emissary Harry Hopkins had assured him that "the President is determined that we shall win the war together". Not until the Japanese declared war on the United States and launched its devastating attack on the Pearl Harbour base on 7th December were Britain and the U.S.A. full allies, but much had happened in secret before that. Throughout 1941 British and U.S. staffs had conferred on forms of co-operation. In March, 1941, American officers visited Britain to select bases for their Atlantic convoy escort vessels and for their air force, and work on these was put in hand at once.(1) Many of the biggest air bases were to be sited in East Anglia, but very few people in the region knew of the plans being made. So great was the work already being done on the expansion of the R.A.F. stations that additional activity was seen as a simple extension of it, without wider significance.

Literally dozens of airfields were under construction simultaneously. It represented one of the biggest civil engineering tasks ever undertaken in the United Kingdom, each of these bases costing as much as £1 million. The construction of a big bomber base typically involved clearing eight miles of hedgerow and 1,500 trees, excavating 400,000 cubic yards of soil, and then laying down ten miles of roads, twenty miles of drains, ten miles of conduit, six miles of water mains and four miles of sewers. The runways required 175,000 cubic yards of concrete, the buildings four and a half million bricks, and the circulating areas 32,000 square yards of tarmac. Typical of a "class A" base of this kind was that at Rougham, near Bury St Edmunds, construction of which was well in hand by the end of 1941. It provided accommodation for 3,000 airmen. Another was at Hardwick, near Bungay.(2)

In March, 1941, the U.S. Congress passed a Lend-Lease Bill so that American arms could continue to be sent to Britain despite the fact that she had no remaining financial resources with which to pay for them. The output of the American munitions factories was split 50-50 between the U.S. forces and the British and Allied forces. By the end of May the British and Canadian navies were able, for the first time, to escort convoys across the whole breadth of the Atlantic; in July merchant shipping sunk on that crossing was reduced to a third of the average loss in the previous five months. On 12th August Churchill and Roosevelt met on board a battleship off the coast of Newfoundland and drew up an "Atlantic Charter" defining the principles of self-government and freedom of choice which they agreed should be the basis of civilised international relations. It was a powerful propaganda boost for Britain, and it was quickly followed by something more practical — Roosevelt ordered his navy to provide escorts over the Newfoundland to Iceland sector for some of the convoys carrying arms to Britain, and he authorised it to attack any Axis ships sighted in "U.S.-interested" waters.

While Britain was thus acquiring allies, there was an unexpected indication that some Germans felt they had problems. In May Hitler's deputy, Rudolf Hess,

Left: The Duke of Kent in the uniform of an R.A.F. group captain talking to A.R.P. workers during a visit to Norwich. The Duke died in an air crash in 1942. *Eastern Daily Press*

Right: The Duke also visited Ipswich, where he is seen inspecting the Felixstowe Road mobile section of the town's medical service.
East Anglian Daily Times

appropriated a German fighter plane and flew himself to Scotland, where he sought to meet British government representatives to talk about the possibility of a peace settlement. The idea was dismissed out of hand and Hess was locked up for the duration.

In the early months of 1941 the British people were frequently enjoined to pray. From 5th January there was "a universal week of prayer", and at the end of March there were special services marking a "National Day of Prayer". Members of the Royal Family, and government ministers when they could be spared from Westminster, visited as many places and talked to as many people as they could, as it was believed that this helped to improve morale. The King and Queen visited the R.A.F. station at Debden during January, the Duke of Kent met civil defence workers in Norwich and Red Cross nurses in Great Yarmouth in April, and in the following month the Duchess of Kent inspected members of the Women's Royal Naval Service (the "Wrens") at their East Coast stations. Among other visitors, the deputy Prime Minister, Clement Attlee, and the Minister of Food, Lord Woolton, visited Norwich.

Jenny Carr's diary contains two entries which show something of the irritations and deprivations of the darkest months of 1941. The first, in January, mentions "the most frightful row with mother" because she had lit a fire with a Christmas card. The family ran a small business and this was the only greetings card they had received from any of their supplying firms, and Jenny had wanted to preserve it as a wartime memento. The other entry, in February, was:

> My birthday today, I am 20. No "happpy returns". Celebration postponed for the duration. Wonder how old I shall be before my coming-of-age can be celebrated. Not too old to enjoy it, I hope.

Not all celebrations were entirely suppressed. When the Hon. Elspeth Ironside, whose father had been Commander-in-Chief of Home Forces during 1940, was married at Narford, near King's Lynn, in February there were two hundred guests at the reception. Three hundred others had been invited, according to newspaper reports, and had been prevented from attending by petrol rationing and other wartime conditions.

During May one of the Mass Observation correspondents spent a few days in a village in East Suffolk, and reported at length. His impression was that general apathy about what was happening in the outside world had increased since his previous visit in July, 1940. He thought there was less interest in the progress of the war, more realisation of the odds against Britain, and a less cheerful atmosphere altogether. But he added that there were:

> No signs of defeatism, nor any crack in morale, but a kind of weary resolution. There may be food trouble, but it wasn't mentioned. There seemed to be unusually few men about, and many girls have also joined the forces. The atmosphere (was). . . . "Something ought to happen somewhere sometime soon, and we're waiting for it, but we are getting bloody tired of this war".[3]

There does not seem to have been any increase in the consumption of alcohol in these difficult times. In fact, West Suffolk Police reported in February a great reduction in drunkenness, and this seems to have reflected the national pattern. Nevertheless, the free churches in Norwich strongly opposed an application to permit public houses to remain open for an extra half-hour (to 10.30 p.m.) during the summer months, and their view prevailed. Ipswich, however, granted the extra time.

Controversy which had flared in 1940 about Sunday opening of cinemas continued well into the new year. In many places, clergymen and ministers resisted the proposal, but usually without success. At King's Lynn the Chief Constable, Mr H.W. Young, welcomed Sunday opening, pointing out that the public houses were open and remarking that "of the two, the cinema was a preferable place for soldiers and young people to attend". The magistrates gave permission, on condition that the entertainment provided was of "a healthy character, and properly conducted", and the cinema agreed to donate seven and a half per cent of its gross takings to the King's Lynn and West Norfolk Hospital. The Bishop of Lichfield had drawn up a list of the films he considered suitable for Sunday showing, and at Mildenhall and Brandon cinemas were allowed to open on Sunday provided they stuck to these films. Newmarket Rural District Council voted eleven to nine not to permit the cinemas at Soham to open on the Sabbath.

For the great majority of people, the cinema and the pub and the radio were the staple entertainments. There were two B.B.C. transmissions, the Home Service and the Forces Programme (The embryonic television transmissions had been suspended at the outbreak of war). Programmes such as "Works Wonders" and "Music while you work", "In Town Tonight", "Any Questions", Tommy Handley's ITMA (It's That Man Again) and "Garrison Theatre" attracted listener loyalty to a degree that has never been surpassed.

There was a widespread effort everywhere to maintain sport and entertainment as usual. Some football was still played; on 15th February Norwich City beat the F.A. Cup holders West Ham 2-1 in the first round of the League War Cup at Carrow Road. There was an attendance of 4,555 and receipts were £240. A week later, in the second leg, played at West Ham, Norwich lost and went out of the competition, but the City team went through to May with an unbroken run of home wins. At Portman Road in June four thousand people watched Norwich City draw 4-4 with an Ipswich XI. When the new season came round, gates were smaller and receipts lower, but just sufficient in the view of the *Eastern Daily Press* to "encourage the Norwich directors in their determination to keep the club in being during the difficult wartime conditions".

The Derby and the Oaks were run at Newmarket. Racing notes still appeared regularly in the *Cambridge Daily News*. Jockeys who had been called up were able without much difficulty to get leave to race during the early part of the year. This changed later and some racing stables in Newmarket found themselves in difficulties. For some tasks they were recruiting men of sixty-five and seventy, and they reported that "some young girls have shown surprising keenness and ability in the saddle". By September all race meetings were confined to Saturdays, and so often clashed. There were some who argued that race meetings were inappropriate during wartime, but the importance of the bloodstock industry was used as full justification for continuing — the sales were held again at Newmarket in October, and over £100,000 changed hands in three days. Earlier in the year when the Home Secretary, Herbert Morrison, had been looking into the matter and had promised Parliament a statement about the future of horseracing, Churchill sent him a hint which was about as subtle as a shovel-blow:

> Will you kindly let me know beforehand what you think of saying? If anything were done which threatened to terminate horse-racing in time of war, or ruin the bloodstock, it would be necessary that the whole matter should be thrashed out in Cabinet first.

So horseracing continued. So did the head of the river races at Cambridge in June. Most of the usual activities, indeed, continued in this university town. Large crowds attended the May Week madrigals. At the Arts Theatre, patrons enjoyed T.S.Eliot's *Murder in the Cathedral* during March, a village drama festival in April, *The Beggar's Opera* and three new ballets in May, Somerset Maugham's *The Constant Wife* in June, Chekhov's *The Cherry Orchard* in October. Emlyn Williams, Marie Tempest, Donald Wolfit and Edith Evans were among the artists who appeared. At the Guildhall one could hear *The Messiah* in April, a programme of Beethoven quartets in May, the London Symphony and the London Philharmonic Orchestras, Dame Myra Hess and Solomon at the piano. In May Mr E.M. Forster lectured on Virginia Woolf, and in November Professor Alfred Richardson attacked modern architecture and declared that most of the planning for post-war London was even then going forward in Cambridge.

Heffers organised an exhibition of the paintings of two nurses working in a nearby R.A.F. hospital and a few months later published *Zuleika in Cambridge,* by S.C. Roberts. The first University Film Society was formed in February. And many drama, music and other cultural groups of all kinds flourished. The *Cambridge Daily News* explained in June that "with the increased population in Cambridge, there is more than ever a need for entertainment in the town".

"Music provides an antidote to war-jaded nerves" said the *Cambridge Daily News* in the caption to this photograph of players and singers at Impington Village College. *Cambridge Daily News*

A big crowd assembled on the Backs behind King's College to listen to the May Week madrigals, a clear indication that in spite of the war life in the university town went on. *Cambridge Daily News*

Other places did not fare so well. The Maddermarket Theatre at Norwich was still fighting the threat of closure because of lack of support, but it opened for a new season (its twentieth) in September with an Irish comedy, *Spring Meeting*. At the Hippodrome and the Theatre Royal the accent was on light entertainment. The *Eastern Daily Press* report of 1st April suggests the flavour of the times:

> Nothing to excel this week's attraction has been seen at the Hippodrome since pre-war days. "Eve on Parade" has been described as London's brightest war-time revue, and it comes to Norwich after a highly successful run at the Garrick Theatre, with a striking selection of its remarkable scenery and beautiful dresses, some first-rate comedians and dancers, and what is probably the largest troupe of glamour girls on tour.

That same week one of the Prime Minister's daughters, Diana Churchill, appeared at the Norwich Theatre Royal in a Frederick Lonsdale comedy, *On Approval.* One of the most popular venues for young people in Norwich, paricularly those in the Forces, was the Lido dance hall, where blind Eddie Gates and his band played through many of the worst air raids on the city.

The smaller towns provided less glamour. Ipswich enjoyed two concerts of popular classics played by the London Philharmonic Orchestra in the Public Hall in September. There were packed audiences, nearly half of which were military, with British and Polish army officers forming a large proportion. At this time, too, a series of extra-mural evening classes began at Ipswich Public Library, and Bernard Newman lectured on "Spies in Fact and Fiction". Bury St Edmunds staged a very successful music festival during May.

People read a lot. The Ipswich Library Committee disclosed in July that during the previous year it had made a record 774,000 issues. There were complaints in Norwich because the public libraries closed during air raids. After 22nd June there was a rush of interest in the war on the Eastern Front and in all things Russian. Young John Rogers in Ipswich wrote in his diary in July:

> I've treated myself to a new book: *William and the Evacuees.*I can't resist this series; I've got them all. I also bought the *Daily Telegraph* War Map of Russia.

When the summer holiday season approached, the government appealed to the public to take holidays at home. Every effort was made throughout the year to discourage people from travelling, but not always successfully. The regulations

Stay-at-home holidays were the rule in 1941, and on August Monday thousands attended specially arranged festivities in Eaton Park at Norwich. *George Swain*

forbidding strangers moving into the coastal Defence Areas were often ignored, and many people were prosecuted. Jenny Carr noted in her diary in March:

> When we got home this afternoon, the G— family from Peterborough, friends of pre-war tennis and bathing summers, had turned up, defying the restrictions. It was jolly to see them all again. We discussed the fun we used to have in "the good old days". Now we are all scattered, all the boys in the war, and it looks as though the girls soon will be . . .

Local authorities in the bigger towns responded to a government request and organised special attractions in their local parks. At Norwich more than a thousand children and parents enjoyed a Whit Monday programme of sports and displays of dancing and physical culture in Eaton Park. Summer attractions were also arranged, and the *Eastern Daily Press* supported the appeal for holidays-at-home:

> Norwich is fortunate in having natural and acquired advantages which, with the aid of social and sports functions of various kinds, should make it an ideal self-contained holiday centre. We hope that these amenities will be fully exploited.

Most people responded. Twenty thousand people attended a gala event in Eaton Park. But, as usual, there were some who did things their own way. Over the three days of August Bank holiday thirty-six extra trains left Liverpool Street station. Most of the passengers they carried did not get through to the coast, but some did. At Cromer Petty Sessions early in September, 160 people were fined for illegally entering the defence area. Fifty-seven of them had travelled from Norwich, fifty-six from other parts of Norfolk, and the remainder from further afield.

Those who lived near the coast were given access to certain limited areas of beach. But for them a carefree holiday mood was scarcely possible. In Sheringham during July Sarah Williams noted:

> Perfect summer weather and in a place like this war seems very remote — until one sees barbed wire on the beach, and planes overhead. Sunday is a quiet day, because there are no army lorries on the roads . . .

Bunty Carr struck a more sombre note in her diary:

> Went to the beach in the afternoon, about 200 yards being open for bathing. Found the entire surrounding villages packed into this small space. Dare not go very far into the water in case of mines, dead bodies, etc.

Towards the end of the year the Eastern Regional Commissioner lifted the ban on visits to the coast, while still urging the public not to travel without good reason.

The enforced and prolonged separation of husbands and wives brought predictable problems. Sarah Williams referred to the subject in July:

> My husband telephoned from Aberdeen. He expects to begin his leave on Thursday. It is five months since I saw him. This war makes us lead lives of unwilling asceticism, and it confirms me in my belief that in renouncing the pleasures of the flesh one forces oneself to place an undue emphasis upon them.

Bathers enjoy the July sunshine at Sheringham, where about 200 yards of beach had been opened, but their leisure was sternly overlooked by a sentry of the 2/5th West Yorkshire Regiment standing guard over the gap in the barbed wire. *Imperial War Museum*

For many the temptations of the flesh were too strong to be resisted, and there were a surprising number of men who went so far as to commit bigamy. Mrs Williams noted:

> A local policeman came into our office today and said a great deal of his work is connected with cases of bigamy.

There were regular prosecutions. A forty-seven-year-old lieutenant who went through a wedding ceremony with a woman at Woodbridge in March was bound over at Suffolk Assizes; a battery sergeant-major with a wife in Sunderland was brought before the Norwich Bench after "marrying" a Norwich woman at St Peter Mancroft in April; and at a later Suffolk Assizes there were four soldiers facing charges of bigamy.

Towards the end of 1941 some battalions began to move overseas and there were large numbers of marriages on the eve of their departure of couples who could not guess how long it would be before they saw one another again — if they ever did. Mrs Williams wrote in her diary:

> Our typist is proposing to get married on Saturday. Her husband-to-be will arrive on Saturday morning and leave on Sunday morning to go overseas, which seems a silly business to me. If they want to sleep together, they ought to do it without all this fuss and bother and the formality of a wedding ceremony. She is only eighteen and doesn't know anything about him or his family. I suspect that the separation allowance has something to do with it.

It seems that her suspicions may have been justified, for another diary entry four days later reads:

> Margaret has at last taken steps to find out whether her sweetheart (whom she should have married today) is married. She is very miserable and was dropping tears all over the typewriter. Poor child!

A week or so after that the subject comes up again in her diary:

> Another case of bigamy in Sheringham. The girl duly "married" is pregnant, and the man has already a wife and four children.

Sarah Williams seems to have studied the sex problems of the time with special attention. Later she returns to the subject:

> The County Assizes opened today and the calendar of cases is a sordid business: rape, murder, infanticide, especially rape. Marion says this is the effect of the war. Some of it is due to the behaviour of the women. I have seen them in Sheringham, thrusting their attentions on soldiers. R— and P— in my office dress in a most provocative manner, but are almost prudish in behaviour. The stimulus is there. I think the way they dress and behave is due largely to the pictures; in fact, by watching R— I can almost tell which film actress is appearing at the local cinema.

There were changes in the boy-meets-girl routine. A Mass Observation report on the state of morale in Ipswich in September, 1941, stated:

> The soldiers have brought with them a gaiety which did not exist in the town's life before. There used to be only cinemas, and a very occasional meeting, which attracted few people. Now one of the cinemas has become a music hall (which it was once before, many years ago) . . . Before the war there were no regular dances in the town; now there is a dance every Monday in the Co-op Hall, and one every Friday in a church hall. I went to the former and was impressed with the small number of civilian men present — only five out of a male attendance of about 100 — and with the comparatively carefree behaviour of the dancers. There was no typical palais-de-dance aloofness, very few girls were dancing together, and there were very few good dancers among the girls . . .
> Before the war youths and girls used to parade the long main shopping street every evening. Now soldiers and girls do the same. Unfortunately, I have no data on what Ipswich male civilians think of this situation. There must be quite a number of them, considering that armaments are made by the local engineering shops. There may be a certain amount of ill-feeling between the two, but what there is is kept well under.[4]

Some local community leaders worried about the young folk. In Bury St Edmunds "frank talks to young people" were organised which were specifically concerned with sexual matters; none too soon, it seems, for the Mayor of Bury had already gone on record as favouring public whipping of boys found guilty of indecent assaults on girls. A Dereham magistrate, commenting on the behaviour of children who had stolen flowers from graves, argued the merits of birching for some offenders. At Ipswich the magistrates ordered four strokes of the birch for two boys, aged twelve and nine, who had stolen while on probation.

There was, indeed, a serious increase in juvenile delinquency during 1941. Early in the year the *Eastern Daily Press* reported that the local juvenile court was unable to find vacancies in any institution for young offenders. The paper commented:

> The problem of the adolescent offender who refuses to co-operate with the leniency of the court is proving apparently insoluble by present methods. Such young people are the despair of judges, recorders, magistrates and court missioners.

Youngsters were sometimes the victims, rather than the perpetrators. The N.S.P.C.C. reported in November an increase in Suffolk in the number of cases of child neglect and in the number of assaults on children. The society brought a number of successful prosecutions: against a Fakenham couple who had been living with their five children in a barn, against a Needham Market woman who neglected five children under seven years of age, against a Gorleston mother whose five children slept in a flea-ridden Anderson shelter and went unwashed for weeks.

In this last case, the mother had been unable to cope on her own, after her husband had been called up. That was not an uncommon state of affairs. But, considering the exceptional tensions and stresses of the time, very few people cracked, even in the darkest period at the beginning of 1941. Very few cases of suicide were reported; the forty-seven-year-old Lowestoft woman who killed herself in February because she worried about air raids and dreaded invasion was quite exceptional.

Winston Churchill publicly warned that a new "invasion season" would begin on 1st September. A Mass Observation report on morale in Ipswich at that time stated:

> There is little fear of a blitz, but the townspeople realise that if there were an invasion, they would immediately be in the thick of it. I was constantly being asked: "What about invasion?", "Do you think he'll invade?", and "What are the chances of Hitler's invading this country?" This also seemed to be a topic of overheard conversation . . . I do not think, from long experience of the habits of Ipswich people, that there is the slightest chance of defeatism becoming a problem in this town. But if invasion *is* attempted, things might be very different. People do not know what to do in that event. They merely know they have to take orders from somebody or other, who will tell them what to do.[5]

A party of war correspondents representing London evening newspapers visited Eastern Command in March and saw, among other things, troops of the 6th Northamptonshire Regiment manning a defence post in the front garden of a Clacton house. *Imperial War Museum*

In the closing months of the year the local Invasion Committees became more active, campaigning against apathy and complacency. The public needed little reminder, however, for in many parts of the region it was able to observe anti-invasion exercises on a more ambitious scale than had ever been attempted before. On 8th October the *Eastern Daily Press* reported:

> The greatest and most comprehensive manoeuvres ever held in this country in peace or war have just been concluded, and thousands of soldiers and armoured vehicles are now back in their war stations. For the purposes of the exercise, it was supposed that the Germans had forced a landing in East Anglia and were attacking in the direction of London.

Six weeks later it carried another report:

> Norfolk has just put its blitz and invasion precautions through searching tests. Military exercises over the weekend gave troops and the Civil Defence services in a large part of the county their first opportunity of collaborating, in preparation to meet any possible enemy surprise.

A fortnight after that there was yet another large-scale exercise. By then it was clear to all that the mobilisation of the nation's resources had reached a new peak. The people had survived a testing year. The tide had turned. Now the forces were being carefully "wound up" for action — and the action would come in partnership with the U.S.S.R., the U.S.A. and the nations of the British Commonwealth. On 1st January, 1941, it had been difficult for anyone to see just how the British could escape defeat. On 31st December, 1941, scarcely anyone doubted the certainty of victory.

CHAPTER EIGHT

Preparing a Punch

WINSTON CHURCHILL sent a memorandum to the Chiefs of Staff Committee on 12th September, 1941, which signalled the opening of a new phase of the war. "An Expeditionary Force equivalent to six divisions should be organised for action overseas," he wrote. "A plan should be prepared to act in whatever is thought to be the best place."[1] Six weeks later Admiral Lord Louis Mountbatten was appointed to the new post of Chief of Combined Operations, charged with the responsibility of planning operations against German-held territory.

Although until this time the government had been primarily concerned to protect the homeland, and the public's attention had focused on what was happening on the European mainland, some British forces had been continuously in action throughout the year. Some of the action had even been in Western Europe. In March British commandos had raided the Lofoten Islands, deep inside the Arctic Circle off the coast of occupied Norway. They had sunk a couple of ships, blown up some fish oil factories, captured 225 prisoners, and brought back 315 Norwegians who wanted to volunteer for the Allied forces. It had been a daring and very successful operation, but no-one could suppose that it was going significantly to affect the course of the war at that period.

The R.A.F. had also been busy. Apart from convoy duty off the East Coast, fighter squadrons from East Anglia had joined in regular attacks on targets on the other side of the Channel. The technique was to despatch a small number of bombers with heavy fighter cover. In the first such raid, in January, No 242 Squadron flying Hurricanes from Martlesham rendezvoused with two squadrons of fighters from North Weald and they escorted half a dozen Blenheim bombers to targets in the Pas de Calais. By the summer these raids had become almost routine and very few bombers were lost. One disaster which came close to home occurred at Honington airfield, near Bury St Edmunds, during May, when a Wellington bomber returning from a night raid attempted to land there with its undercarriage retracted. The plane slewed to one side and crashed into the main bomb dump, where it burst into flames. Two members of the crew were saved by the efforts of two officers at the station, both of whom were awarded the George Medal.[2]

Usually four Lancaster or Halifax four-engined heavy bombers or a squadron of Blenheims, flying at 12,000 feet, were accompanied on these raids by thirty-six

Troops building a kapok infantry bridge at Dunmow, Essex, during their training.
Imperial War Museum

Spitfires, which flew above them in formation to about 20,000 feet. This formation came to be known as "the beehive", because that is exactly what it looked like as it crossed the sky. These raids had a dual purpose, to destroy factories that were working for the Germans and to destroy Luftwaffe fighters. Later, they had the additional value that they forced the Germans to keep planes in the west which might otherwise have been moved to the Russian front. Important as this aerial activity was, however, it could have only a very limited effect on the course of war.

It was during one of these raids, in August, that Wing Commander Douglas Bader's Spitfire collided with a Messerschmitt Bf 109 in mid-air. He lost his artificial legs in this incident, but within a matter of weeks had acquired a new pair, flown from Horsham St Faiths, near Norwich, and dropped by parachute on to the German-occupied airfield at St Omer-Longeunesse.

The main scene of Allied action was in the Mediterranean area — in Africa, in Greece and on the islands of Crete and Malta. Before the war Mussolini had sought to build a far-flung Italian empire in Africa and until the end of 1940 the Axis operations in that theatre had been left to the Italians. In September, 1940, they had advanced into Egypt, but three months later, when Allied forces counter-attacked, the Italians began a full-scale retreat. Their army of ten divisions was virtually destroyed, and 130,000 of them were taken prisoner, with nearly 400 tanks and 850 guns. The R.A.F. attacked the Italian airfields and the Royal Navy bombarded ports and coastal roads. Australian and New Zealand troops were heavily engaged in these operations. Newspaper headlines announcing the capture of Bardia, Tobruk and Benghazi provided almost the only encouraging news of that dark winter. Some of the troops stationed at Colchester heard the news of the fall of Benghazi to Allied forces directly from the lips of Winston Churchill — he was there when the news came through, visiting the battalion of the Royal Scots Fusiliers which he had commanded in the First World War. There were other successes in East Africa, where the Italians were defeated in Abyssinia and Somaliland and driven out of the Sudan.

By that time, however, the Germans had turned their attention southward. Luftwaffe squadrons were posted to southern Italy and Sicily before the end of 1940 — there were 250 German planes in Sicily by the end of January. They bombed the British base in Malta almost ceaselessly, three or four times every day, from January to June, and attacked shipping carrying supplies and reinforcements to Allied forces in Africa. Nevertheless, by early March an Allied strategic reserve of four divisions had been built up in Egypt. The Germans then stepped up the pressure. In mid-February they had sent the formidable Afrika Korps, commanded by Lieutenant General Erwin Rommel, to help the Italians. At the end of March Rommel launched his attack and, in less than a fortnight, he drove the Allied forces from almost all the territory they had captured from the Italians. He failed, however, to take Tobruk by assault.

Early in April the Germans invaded Yugoslavia and Greece. This move had been

A Bristol Blenheim IV being loaded with bombs ready for a sweep over the Channel in the summer of 1941. *East Anglian Daily Times*

foreseen and a substantial number of British, Australian and New Zealand troops had moved from Egypt into Greece, but the German advance proved irresistable; Yugoslavia surrendered on the eleventh day and the Greek Army on the fifteenth, and the Allied forces had to try to get out quickly, without air cover. During the last week of April about 43,000 men escaped, but 11,000 were left behind, as well as a vast amount of equipment. There followed a fierce and bloody battle for the island of Crete, to which most of the Allied troops had retreated. It was all over in a few days, due to the Germans' vastly superior air strength. About 2,000 British seamen were killed or wounded. The Germans, for their part, lost 6,000 soldiers and airmen killed, wounded or posted missing.

Thus when the Prime Minister sent his memorandum to the Chiefs of Staff in September the war had entered a completely new phase. The Germans occupied virtually the whole of Europe and had a strong and threatening presence in North Africa and the Mediterranean. Although Japan was not yet involved in the War, there were anxieties about the situation in the Far East. Since May the Chief of the Imperial General Staff had been urging the reinforcement of Singapore, but

Churchill refused to weaken the Middle East strength. On the Eastern Front the Russians, who had been ill-prepared for the Nazi invasion on 22nd June, had suffered enormous losses and had fallen back rapidly, so that the Germans had captured Smolensk, were attacking Kiev and had isolated Leningrad. According to one distinguished war historiam: "In London and Washington the belief was that the campaign would be over in a few months at the most".[3] Then the Germans might try to cross the Caucasus and push south towards Suez and the Persian Gulf.

The brightest hope was that the United States would soon decide to join the Allied cause in an active fighting role. Meanwhile, the British people were urged to make even greater efforts. More men were called up, and women were exhorted to take a more active role. The Ministry of Labour and National Service estimated in August that it would be necessary to withdraw one million men from industry and to redistribute two and a quarter million men and women to the Army and Civil Defence. By the autumn "the strategic slant of the war economy was changing;

Left: Members of the A.T.S. working with a heavy anti-aircraft battery. In the foreground is the central control post, and in the background are A.T.S. girls at work on a height-finder.
East Anglian Daily Times

Right: An advertisement issued by the Ministry of Labour and National Service directed to the women of Essex.
East Anglian Daily Times

Below: Deputy Premier Mr Clement Attlee and his wife visiting a "shop window factory" in a Cambridge store in which munitions factory work was being demonstrated.
Cambridge Daily News

'If only all you women would help'

Call personally, or post this to
THE WAR WORK OFFICE
HIGH STREET, COLCHESTER,
or to the
EMPLOYMENT EXCHANGE,
EAST STOCKWELL STREET,
COLCHESTER.

I wish to join the A.T.S. or offer my services for War Work. My present job is ______
and my age ______

WHAT SHOULD I DO?

Name ______
Address ______

NEXT WEEK IS COLCHESTER'S WAR WEEK

Your men . . . the men of Essex, have already answered the call, you **women** must help them!

. . . . the A.T.S. need 30,000 women and girls, the factories are crying out for women workers, do not let anyone hold you back . . . ENROL TODAY!

HERE ARE TWO IMMEDIATE NEEDS

IN THE A.T.S. Splendid openings are waiting for you. In radiolocation . . . on Ack-Ack batteries . . . or on secret devices. You can make secret drawings, transmit messages, undertake confidential secretarial work. Exciting jobs for drivers — splendid openings in office work — first class training in cooking, catering and dietetics. And it's a wonderful life. Good holidays . . . good billets . . . good food and good pay. Your work is needed, appreciated and well rewarded.

IN THE WAR FACTORIES. Fascinating jobs are waiting. Delicate precision work, important inspection work, office jobs where initiative is needed . . . welfare work. All to have arms piling up in the arsenals, ships ready for slipways, planes waiting in hangars. Go straight to a job, or take a deeply interesting course at a Training Centre. You're paid while you train (with allowances for dependants) and wonderfully looked after. It's an absorbing, happy life!

Part time work.

EMPLOYERS. *Are you making full use of Part Time Workers? There are many ready to help you NOW. Ask at the Ministry of Labour and National Service.*

TO WOMEN. *Don't worry if you can't do Full Time war work. You can register now for part time work. Ask at the War Work Office High Street, or at the Employment Exchange, East Stockwell Street.*

There is a place for every woman in

★ ★ CALL PERSONALLY OR WRITE TO THE **WAR WORK OFFICE**, HIGH STREET, OR EMPLOYMENT EXCHANGE, EAST STOCKWELL STREET, COLCHESTER

Issued by the Ministry of Labour and National Service

preparedness to meet the attack and hold the line was giving way to active preparations for the offensive".[4]

In September all men between eighteen and sixty were required to register for Civil Defence duties, after which they were liable for forty-eight hours' duty a month. In December it was announced that all men aged eighteen-and-a-half to fifty were liable to be called up to the armed forces, and from January,1942, all single women aged twenty to thirty had the choice of joining one of the women's auxiliary services or taking a job in a war factory. Younger men who had been in "reserved occupations" now found themselves "de-reserved" and were quickly put into uniform.

Youngsters were drawn in, too, although not compulsorily. From the beginning of the year those between sixteen and eighteen had been urged to join the Air Training Corps, which prepared them for service in the R.A.F., especially as pilots and other aircrew. Four squadrons were formed in Norwich and the response was good everywhere. Nine Suffolk squadrons were represented at a sports meeting at Woodbridge in September. There was also a new Youth Service Corps, which recruited a wider range — from fourteen to twenty — for a variety of work.

The direct involvement of women in the war effort raised a certain amount of controversy, which began even before any element of compulsion was introduced. Women were employed in a whole range of jobs which hitherto had been done by men — some of them worked on the construction of the new airfields in East

Some of the hundred women and girls who were helping to construct an airfield "somewhere in East Anglia".
Eastern Daily Press

The Mayor of Ipswich, Mr R. F. Jackson, inspecting members of the Air Training Corps after opening an A.T.C. recruiting centre in Ipswich.
East Anglian Daily Times

Anglia, helping to lay storm pipes. For a sixty hour week they were paid from £3 5s. to £4 15s, very good wages compared with anything they might earn elsewhere; so good, in fact, that there were protests. Farmers pointed out that they could not compete at that level. The Carr family lost an employee from their garage in Norfolk, and Jenny Carr noted in her diary:

> W—, our mechanic, asked this morning if he might leave on Saturday without notice, as he has the chance of a job with constructors at the aerodrome, wiring or something, at £4 13s. a week. That is twice what we can afford to pay him, so he is leaving.

Another diarist, Cecil Sparks, the special constable who lived near Norwich, had strong views on this subject. He wrote, in an entry towards the end of 1941:

> Talking to a man today who lives near an aerodrome in this county, he told me of one or two instances which had come to his notice of the extremely high wages being paid to very unskilled labour. One boy, aged 14, was receiving £3 0s.7d. a week, and a girl £4 5s. a week, plus all expenses to and from her work. He also spoke of older men getting high wages for virtually nothing.
>
> Surely in this pernicious state of affairs lie the seeds of many evils? Isn't it a preliminary to inflation? Can't it be the reason why the A.T.S. are crying out for girls? Isn't it why a lot of people (as in the last war) want this war to go on indefinitely? . . . The real cause of all the trouble appears to be the "cost plus profit" basis upon which the contractors are paid. Of course they will not do anything to keep costs down as long as their profits are assessed on the cost of the job they undertake. It is about time the government knew what these jobs *should* cost, and high time they paid accordingly.

Returning to the employment of women, many were working in forestry in the region, there were a lot in the local factories, and as 1941 began there were a good many working on buses. The Eastern National Omnibus Company found itself in trouble early in the year when it proposed to split up some bus crews because "complaints had been made that some of the drivers had become friendly with conductresses, where they had worked on the same bus for several months". A strike was only just averted. Some passengers also behaved differently when there

'BUS DRIVERS
AND
"FARE GIRLS"

MUST NOT GET TOO FRIENDLY

"SPLITTING UP" ORDER AT CHELMSFORD

Women 'bus conductors employed by the Eastern National Omnibus Co. at Chelmsford wish to retain the system which has been in operation up to now whereby they always go out on 'buses with the same drivers. Company, with

Left: How the local newspapers reported the controversy surrounding teamwork by bus crews in Essex. *East Anglian Daily Times*

Right: Some women seem to have been all too eager to get to grips with the enemy—a still from a newsreel film about the Littleport War Weapons Week. *East Anglian Film Archive*

was a conductress on duty. A Norwich woman who was turned away from a bus because it was full slapped the conductress's face; she was prosecuted for assault. When Ernest Bevin, the Minister of Labour and National Service, visited Norwich in August he used tough language about the contribution required from women, and threatened action against any of them who left their jobs. The message was generally understood to be intended for women without children, but some mothers did take employment. The annual report for 1941 of the School Medical Officer for the City and County of Norwich was highly critical of them. He said he wished "to protest with the utmost vigour at my command against the employment of women who have children", adding:

> I am in no position to express any opinion on the country's needs for labour, and it may be necessary to employ such women, but in my view they ought not to be allowed to go out to work until every other source of labour has been utterly exhausted, and that certainly has not occurred yet.

This view was not universally shared. When Cambridge staged a "War Work Week" early in October to coax women into the Services or the factories, there were complaints that there was no day nursery in the town where mothers could leave young children, and that the six nursery schools in the town were all full. The chairman of the Maternity and Child Welfare Committee said the Ministry of Health had been asked to provide three prefabricated buildings, so that greater provision could be made.

In February the Bury St Edmunds Watch Committee refused to appoint a woman police constable, although the example had been set in other parts of the country. When the new engineering block of the Norwich City College was brought into use in August, a large part of it was given over to a two-month training course in fitting and turning, and almost all the places were taken by women and girls on their way to employment in war factories. By October the postal authorities in Norwich found it impossible to recruit a single male, and postwomen appeared for the first time. The *Norfolk and Norwich Weekly Press* reported:

> Each woman goes on two deliveries a day, the hours being from 5.30 a.m. to 5.30 p.m., or 6.20 a.m. to 7.35 p.m., with a break for a meal between deliveries . . . Very shortly the women will be provided with uniforms, which will consist of slacks or skirt, whichever is preferred, jacket, and a peaked cap. So far, the postwomen have been very well received by the public.

Jenny Carr mentioned in her diary an odd anxiety of some of the younger women who were required to register:

> Girls worried because men will find out our ages by asking if we have registered yet . . .

So, as the year progressed, everyone was drawn into the net. But the war effort needed more equipment, as well as more human beings. And more equipment called for an increased supply of raw materials. So a campaign to salvage suitable materials, which had started in 1940, was stepped up. Churches, colleges and public buildings of every kind were denuded of their railings and other ironwork, the railings from the County Hall in Ipswich, for example, being removed in February. In May the Cambridge Shire Hall lost its railings, and the council resolved that those around Parker's Piece should go. Southwold Town Council drew the government's attention to the derelict Southwold Railway, which had closed down in 1929, and urged that its rails be used for munitions. The City Hall at Norwich kept intact its bronze doors and guardian lion figures, and it was not entirely clear whether a letter published in the *Eastern Daily Press* in October was intended to be taken seriously. It purported to have been written by the lions and it read:

> Having heard that the city is to be combed for surplus railings and metal, we have agreed, together with the grotesques on the bronze doors, to ask you to plead that we may be allowed to join in the national effort — particularly as we feel that our Nazi salutes are inopportune at the present time.

Metals of all kinds were the most sought after raw materials, but it was recognised that almost everything was capable of being recycled. Foil, paper, rags and bones were among the other things collected. Propaganda films were made to stimulate the search; in the Blofield and Flegg district, east of Norwich, villagers were not allowed to go to the film shows unless they turned up with a bundle of rags or a pile of newspapers. Boy Scouts played a big part in collecting and sorting the waste paper; in Cambridge they collected 200 tons during the year.

A Supermarine Spitfire fighter paid for by the Norfolk branch of the National Farmers' Union and therefore named *The Norfolk Farmer*. *Eastern Daily Press*

In January the Ministry of Supply made a general appeal to the public to donate any binoculars they possessed, and the gentlemen of East Anglia came forward patriotically with a large number of them.

The government had another major concern, to cut to the minimum the demand for consumer goods of every kind. Rationing and other controls had done this to a large extent, but this was now reinforced by an effort to take as much money as possible out of circulation. This was done by encouraging saving, and the propaganda was designed to suggest that the scale of war production would be directly related to the amounts saved. Economics were not widely understood at the time.

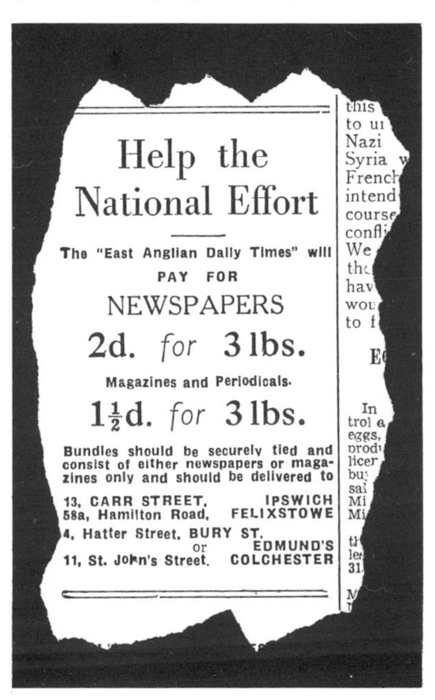

Local newspapers played their part in organising the waste paper salvage drive.
East Anglian Daily Times

The Norfolk branch of the National Farmers' Union was told in August that the £6,347 it had collected had paid for a Spitfire, leaving some over towards the cost of a second plane. Saffron Walden announced in December that it was going to raise £120,000 to buy a corvette for the Navy. "Don't Spend — Lend" was the popular slogan. Tanks and guns were taken around the region for the many special Savings Weeks that were organised; contingents from the armed services and civil defence were sometimes on parade.

The amounts that were raised were spectacular. Cambridge announced at the end of June that it had contributed over £4,000,000 in eighteen months; by November the total ran above £5,000,000. In that month there was a special Warship Week and Cambridge raised a further £700,000, which it was said was the cost of a destroyer. So as not to have to wait until one was built with the money, the

WHICH IS INC... RATED THE ... IPSWIC... EXPRESS

IPSWICH, WEDNESDAY, JUNE 18, 1941

RADIOLOCATION IS BRITAIN'S NEW AIR WEAPON

RAYS UNAFFECTED BY FOG OR DARKNESS DETECT RAIDERS

ONE OF BEST KEPT SECRETS OF WAR NOW REVEALED

CALL FOR TEN THOUSAND MEN AND LARGE NUMBER OF WOMEN AS OPERATORS

Radiolocation, a secret method of detecting raiders by day or night, and a weapon which played a big part in the Battle of Britain, was revealed to the world last night by Air Chief Marshal Sir Philip Joubert.

The system has been one of the best-kept secrets of the war. Even in the Services it has been referred to only by three letters, and even these could not be whispered outside.

Briefly it is a system whereby rays which are unaffected by fog or darkness are sent out [illegible]yond our shores. Any aircraft or ship in the path of this ray sends back a signal to the [illegible] station, where a permanent watch is kept.

Men, it was stated yesterday, with a knowledge of radio work are urgently needed. The im[illegible] [illegible] of the three [illegible] total about 10,000 men [illegible] number of women.

Radar had already played a vital role in the Battle of Britain when the fact of its existence was made public in June, 1941. Developed largely at Orfordness and Bawdsey in the years before the outbreak of war, radar—or radiolocation as it was originally termed—enabled early warning of air activity to be given to Fighter Command operations rooms such as that shown above, staffed largely by members of the Women's Auxiliary Air Force. The public announcement in June was made in conjuction with an appeal for men with a knowledge of radio work and women to join the forces.

East Anglian Daily Times

Stowmarket Home Guard is inspected by Captain W. G. Fallowfield, R. N., when the town's War Weapons Week began on 31st March.

town decided to adopt one already in service, H.M.S. *Loyal.* Everyone seems to have had a jolly time in the process of collecting the cash. There was an admiral to open the proceedings, with naval cadet buglers; there were parades of Servicemen and women on Parker's Piece, and a special church service; there was an exhibition in the Corn Exchange which included a replica mine made of solid silver, a whole array of genuine weapons including torpedoes, guns and mines, a German U-boat periscope, an R.A.F. gun turret, and much else. And there was a dance at the Rex Ballroom to round off the programme.

Sometimes captured German planes were put on display, as at Gayton, near King's Lynn, in June, when a Messerschmitt Bf 109 was displayed on the Crown Meadow and the public paid sixpence a time to inspect it. Enthusiasm was very successfully generated, the propaganda side of the exercise being handled with great skill. As War Weapons Week began in Bury St Edmunds with a service in the cathedral, the target was fixed at £150,000. When it was announced that the sum actually raised was £372,313, morale was given a boost all round. Similarly, Halesworth announced a target of £8,000 ("the cost of four torpedoes"), and actually collected £33,944. Stowmarket went for £20,000 in the week — and

announced that it had raised £27,000 on the first day. Newmarket was particularly modest about its aim — £20,000; afterwards it claimed to have raised over £260,000. Much-battered Lowestoft and Lothingland chipped in with no less than £397,525. An amazing level of achievement was reported from all sides. The tiny village of Sustead, near Cromer, with only 110 inhabitants somehow raised £6,202, an average of £56 a head.

The people who contributed so freely were able to see with their own eyes the way in which production of weapons was being increased. Armoured fighting vehicles seemed to be everywhere in East Anglia. They were seen trundling through towns and villages in convoy, or being carried into the area by the trainload, and occasionally someone travelling away from home would glimpse large concentrations of tanks on the heathlands. In September King George VI, accompanied by his brother, the Duke of Gloucester, and by the Commander-in-Chief of Home Forces, General Sir Alan Brooke, inspected the 6th Armoured Division at Brandon, Suffolk, and the Valentine Mark III tanks were lined up as far as the eye could see, far too many to count.

Left: Tanks as far as the eye can see: Valentine Mk III tanks of the 6th Armoured Division lined up on the Breckland near Brandon for inspection by King George VI.
Imperial War Museum

Right: A 12-inch railway gun of No 9 Super Heavy Regiment, Royal Artillery, on its special siding alongside the Ipswich-Felixstowe railway line at Trimley Heath. The track is covered by camouflage netting.
Imperial War Museum

About this time, some residents near the coast became aware of the presence of the 9th Super Heavy Regiment of the Royal Artillery, who were responsible for 12-inch howitzers mounted on railway well-wagons. These guns weighed 80 tons apiece and fired 750lb shells to a maximum range of 16,500 yards. One of them was sited about a mile east of Nacton, and another on Trimley Heath. The Nacton gun was hidden by a copse of fir trees — until it fired some practice shots and defoliated them! The other was kept well hidden in a big shed, the top of which could be run back on rails to leave the gun exposed. These weapons were specifically intended to deal with invaders, being able to drop shells offshore anywhere between the Cork lightship and Harwich Harbour — a few practice shots were tried. Doubtless, they would have done great damage to landing craft if any had appeared there. They also had Martlesham Heath airfield within range, and could have shelled it if ever paratroopers had sought to land there.(5)

There were many other signs of Britain's growing strength. By the autumn of 1941, there could be no question that the nation was mobilised for war to the utmost degree. It was clear to everyone that soon there would be action.

CHAPTER NINE

Courage and Resolution

SOME OF the most dramatic events of the war occurred during the last three months of 1941: the German army besieged Leningrad, reached the outskirts of Moscow, and advanced into the Crimea; the Japanese bombed Pearl Harbour, crippling the U.S. Pacific Fleet, and invaded the Malay Peninsula, Hong Kong, the Philippines, Burma and Borneo; the United States declared war on Japan, Germany and Italy; and the British launched a major offensive against Rommel's forces in North Africa.

Until Nazi Germany invaded the Soviet Union, the two countries had had a non-aggression pact. The new situation, therefore, called for a sudden and spectacular change of attitude towards Russia on the part of the British government and people. A correspondent of the *Eastern Daily Press* raised some awkward questions in a letter published on 2nd September. How could the Russians be so

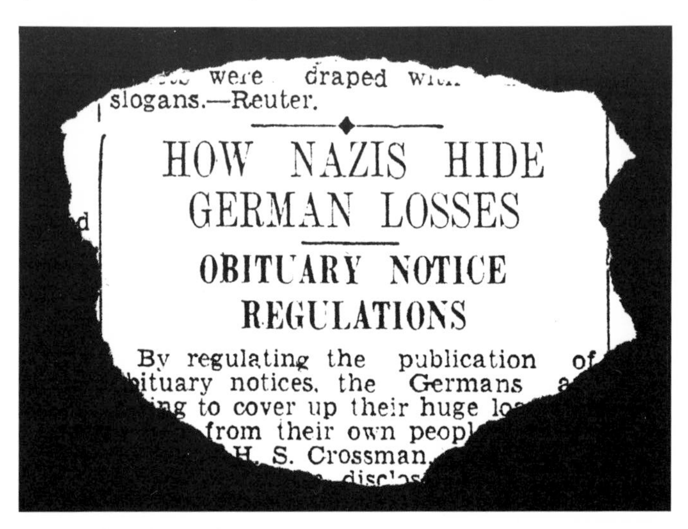
slogans.—Reuter.

HOW NAZIS HIDE GERMAN LOSSES

OBITUARY NOTICE REGULATIONS

By regulating the publication of [illegible]ituary notices, the Germans [illegible] to cover up their huge lo[illegible] from their own peop[illegible] S. Crossman

British propaganda which was primarily aimed at lowering German morale could also be used to raise the morale of Britons on the Home Front.
East Anglian Daily Times

brave, heroic and resourceful, he inquired, when only a few months earlier they had been described as half-starved animals, devoid of decency, and confirmed cowards when they had been fighting the Finns? Had the public been misinformed one way or the other? he asked.

The Conservative M.P. for Norwich, Mr H.G. Strauss, told the House of Commons that he thought it right "to let bygones be bygones" and to help Russia in the fight against "the greatest menace to the world"; but he thought it would be a mistake to say things which would do Britain harm in the world just because Russia was fighting Germany. This presumably meant, when decoded, that old anti-Communist views should be put in cold storage but would not be abandoned. The *Eastern Daily Press* editorialised under the heading "Our Enemy's Enemies". There were political differences, there was no contractual obligation, but Britain should give unqualified support to Russia, it argued.

Most of the general public seemed to take a different view. On the day after Germany invaded Russia, Bunty Carr reported of her North Norfolk village:

> Everyone cheerful today about Russia. Evacuees very pleased.

A few people seem to have been pleased for the wrong reasons. Mrs Sarah Williams, in Sheringham, noted in her diary during August:

> Some female arrived at the office and said she was delighted to see Russia and Germany fighting each other, because they would each be worn out and therefore neither a danger to the Empire.

Cecil Sparks, living just outside Norwich, represented a different school of thought. He wrote in his diary in mid-September:

> It is good to hear that an R.A.F. wing has arrived in Russia. But let us hope we are doing a lot more for them than we hear of. I am perfectly certain we are only told "what is good for us" when the Ministry of Information think the time is ripe.

By mid-December Mrs Williams was recording that:

> Everywhere the main remark about the war seems to be "Aren't the Russians doing well." I think, for me, the change of attitude towards the Russians is best illustrated by Miss A—. She was a real Tory, and hadn't a good word to say about the Russians. They were atheists, baby-murderers, polygamists, etc., etc. But all this week she has been going round from house to house in the town selling flags for Russia. It is really incredible.

What impressed every reasonable man and woman was the fierce patriotism and dogged courage of the Russians. Though the German onslaught drove them out of vast areas of their country, brought the occupation of some of their big cities, and caused terrible loss of life, they showed no sign of cracking. They adopted a "scorched earth" policy, burning to the ground the towns and villages they were forced to surrender to the invaders. If army units became separated from the main force, they continued to fight as independent guerilla groups. And, in the depth of a desperately cold winter which froze the Germans in their tracks, the Red Army counter-attacked and inflicted great damage. By Christmas the Germans had suffered three-quarters of a million casualties and the German long-range bomber force had been blunted.

During this early phase of the Russo-German war there was not a lot that Britain could do to help. Some tanks and aircraft were diverted and by the end of the year eight convoys to Archangel and Murmansk had been organised by the Royal Navy.

But there was intense public interest, and debate. The fortunes of the Russian forces were followed closely. Sarah Williams noted at one moment in October when the picture looked black:

> A better day as far as the weather is concerned, but the depression concerning Russia continues. In the doctor's waiting room people were talking about it, hoping the Russians would be able to hold out. As one man said: "If the Russians have to give in, we might as well do the same. If the Russians can't withstand the Germans, how can we?" This seems to be very much the general sentiment.

By that time there was general agreement in the country that as Britain and Soviet Russia found themselves cast as allies, it was very much in Britain's interest to behave as an unqualified ally. The Deputy Prime Minister, Clement Attlee, visited Norwich in October to speak on the theme "Russia's struggle is our struggle". An Anglo-Soviet Friendship Committee was formed there soon afterwards, and similar committees were quickly established almost everywhere. In

Aid to Russia came in many forms, and even greyhounds could help the war effort. *Eastern Daily Press*

Ipswich the Mayor and Corporation attended a service of intercession for Russia at St Mary-le-Tower Church and this was followed by an Anglo-Russian fortnight. John Rogers bought tickets in an Ipswich draw and won a prize—"three books about Russia". The Theatre Royal in Norwich put on an Anglo-Russian Circus show, and the Maddermarket Theatre staged a "Russian Week", while Boundary Park greyhound stadium gave its net gate receipts to the Aid for Russia Fund. The hammer and sickle appeared in whitewash on walls.

Britain's main preoccupation, meanwhile, was with North Africa and the Mediterranean. The German siege of Tobruk continued, but in September a convoy got through with 6,000 Australian troops and 2,000 tons of supplies. In October British commandos landed from submarines to make a daring raid on Rommel's headquarters; they killed a number of officers, but Rommel was away at the time. By November the Eighth Army in the Western Desert had grown to be the largest body of armour which Britain had ever assembled anywhere and was ready for action. On the 18th it launched its attack, anticipating by a few days a planned German drive towards Egypt. The fighting was fierce and often confused, but in mid-December Rommel pulled back those of his forces which had advanced, except for 15,000 at and near Bardia, who were left to be taken prisoners in the New Year. As the year ended, however, the Eighth Army had failed in its objective to destroy the Axis armies in North Africa.

These battles were well reported and closely followed by the public, but the fact that British forces were now in large-scale action did not raise high hopes. John Rogers wrote in his diary towards the end of November:

> On train to Ipswich with an airman going home for a weekend's leave, I had an interesting talk. He feels quite pleased about the news from Libya, but can't quite see how it can help the war and Russia. I feel the same myself.

Russia suffered enormous casualties as the Germans advanced to the gates of Moscow, and the help given by the British Red Cross Society and the Order of St John of Jerusalem must have helped to alleviate the suffering a little.
East Anglian Daily Times

November and December brought news of cruel blows to the Royal Navy. In November the aircraft carrier *Ark Royal* was torpedoed by a U-boat after it had delivered Hurricane fighters to Malta, and the battleship *Barham* was sunk by another U-boat off the Shetlands, with the loss of 861 lives. On 10th December Japanese aircraft bombed and sank the battle cruiser *Repulse* and a new battleship, the *Prince of Wales,* off the east coast of Malaya, and 800 sailors were lost. Then, on 19th December, the battleships *Queen Elizabeth* and *Valiant* were severely damaged when Italian frogmen clamped explosive charges to their hulls while they were lying at Alexandria, and the same day some smaller vessels based at Malta ran into an Italian minefield and suffered badly.

John Rogers recorded in his diary his shock at the loss of the two vessels in the Far East, but added:

> I have read about the war with Japan without surprise, but I did find it sudden. Most people felt this way. Realised it would make it worse for us, but we will win in the end.

Sarah Williams reported similar confidence among her Sheringham contacts:

> Discussion of the Far Eastern situation. The general feeling was: "Yes, the news is bad, but this is probably according to plan, because we always lose the first battle and win the last". I retorted that that was all right if the first battle wasn't also the last, as in the case of France . . .

There were many families in East Anglia who had a direct personal interest in the war which had now broken out in the Far East. Early in October the men of the 18th Division were issued with khaki drill and ordered to prepare for overseas posting[(1)]. There were embarkation leaves, innoculations, special church services, and visits to various units by King George VI. The men embarked between 28th and 31st October, some at Liverpool and some in the Clyde, and then crossed a foggy Atlantic in convoy. The 1st Suffolks were on board the liner *Orcades,* the 2nd battalion on the Polish motor vessel *Sobieski*, the 4th battalion on the s.s. *Andes*, the 5th on the s.s.*Reina del Pacifico,* and so on. Altogether there were 15,000 men of the Royal Norfolk, Suffolk and Cambridgeshire regiments. British destroyers accompanied them half way across the Atlantic, and the U.S. Navy then took over and saw them safely to Halifax, in Nova Scotia. There they transshipped to American vessels which provided much better accommodation, the former luxury liner *America* among them. The new convoy sailed southwards, halted briefly in the West Indies, continued down the coast of South America, and then crossed to Cape Town, arriving on 9th December. There were four days ashore, route-marching every morning, but free for sightseeing the rest of the time.

During those days at the Cape men learned that Japan had entered the war, that the vital British naval base of Singapore was under threat, and that the *Prince of Wales* and the *Repulse* had been lost off Malaya. But they still did not know where they would end their voyage. It might be Singapore, or it might be Egypt. The troopships sailed from Cape Town on 13th December, out into the Indian

Ocean. Some of them, including those carrying the 1st and 2nd Suffolks, put into Mombasa on Christmas Day and the men had three days ashore. It was extremely hot, there was little to do but swim, and many of them ended up with severe sunburn. Other vessels sailed straight to Bombay, and on these traditional American fare was served on Christmas Day: roast turkey, braised Virginia ham, candied carrots. The men disembarked at Bombay on 28th December, and travelled by train over the Western Ghats to Ahmednagar, where they encamped. Thus, during the closing days of the year, thousands of men from East Anglia found themselves fully trained and fully armed, far from home, en route to a battlefield, but they did not know which one. Nor did they know that within a matter of weeks they would all be prisoners of the Japanese.

Back at home, the families of these men did not know at Christmas where they were. Even for those who were in touch with their men in the forces, it was a Christmas of forced gaiety. Sarah Williams' husband was in the Shetlands, and so relatively safe, but after she had sat down with her young son to a dinner of roast chicken and Christmas pudding she wrote in her diary:

> Even food doesn't taste the same without him here. We listened a lot to the wireless . . .

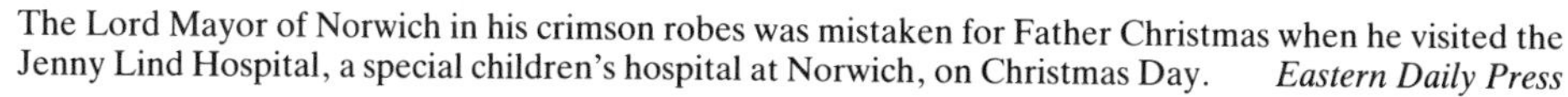
The Lord Mayor of Norwich in his crimson robes was mistaken for Father Christmas when he visited the Jenny Lind Hospital, a special children's hospital at Norwich, on Christmas Day. *Eastern Daily Press*

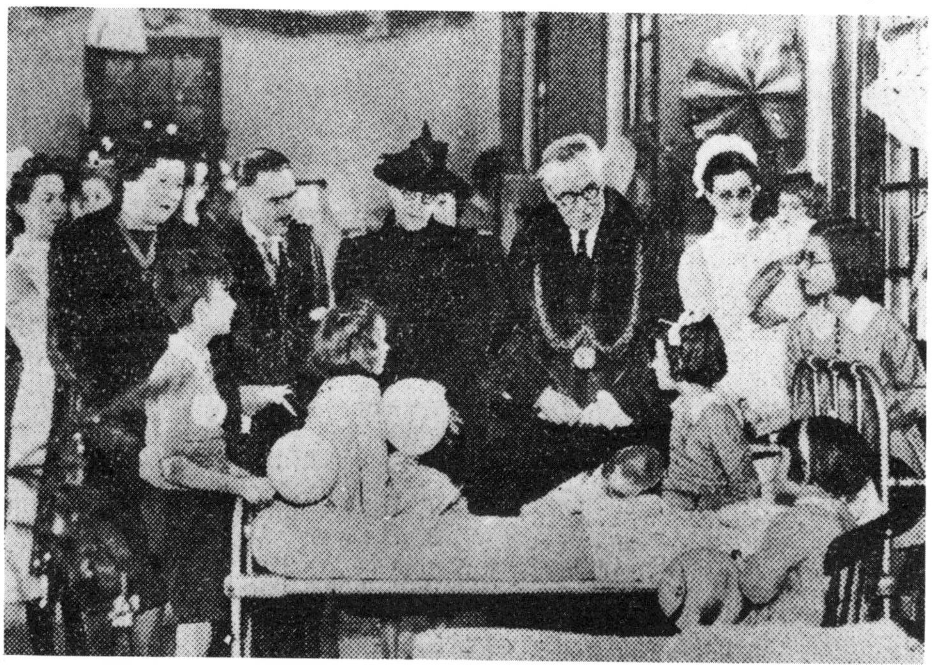

Young John Rogers in Ipswich found the usual Christmas Day routine badly upset:

> Father had to firewatch from 11.30 to 2 p.m., so Christmas dinner was a bit late, but nevertheless enjoyable . . . I went on fire-watching at business at 7 p.m. for all-night duty. I did not feel too pleased. The evening passed quite pleasantly; table tennis had been rigged up and I had a few good games. We had arranged to make a "do" of this night, and all had contributed a little something. We had fried sausages, fried onions and boiled potatoes. Mr R— brought plum pie his wife had made. There were cups of tea, and beer for those who wanted it . . .

Cecil Sparks, near Norwich, philosophized a little in his diary:

> Christmas Day this year was very like peacetime ones, save that the families were not complete; some far away we hope to have with us next year, others can never attend another earthly Christmas. To them we owe more than we can ever pay. The children helped to make Christmas this year. Rations had been eked out over the last few weeks,

and so we were able to make the table look something like pre-war days. This is a splendid achievement for Lord Woolton's Food Ministry. I wonder what the people in Germany had. We all listened to H.M. the King this afternoon (on the radio). I think it a good thing that there should be such a broadcast, even if the subject matter is stereotyped, as it is bound to be.

The minimal festivities concluded, everyone went back to work without delay to face the grim realities. Jenny Carr, by this time working as a land girl on a farm in Suffolk, described her journey back from Norfolk:

> I caught the 3 p.m. train. It was packed. I stood in a sprawling mass of soldiers, evacuees, relations, and local people, wedged in the corridor of a very long train much too long for the stations . . . The Christmas recess now seems like a pleasant dream. Christmas at home never seemed so sweet before since I was a kid.

Now, as one of the darkest years in Britain's history drew to a close, people cast their minds back over its grim events, and felt grateful simply to have survived.

Left: Field-Marshal Lord Ironside, the former C-in-C, Home Forces, inspecting the school Officers Training Corps when he visited Framlingham College for speech day in October. *East Anglian Daily Times*

Right: A huge mound of barley spilled out across the road when bombs hit a maltings in the Ipswich dock area. *East Anglian Daily Times*

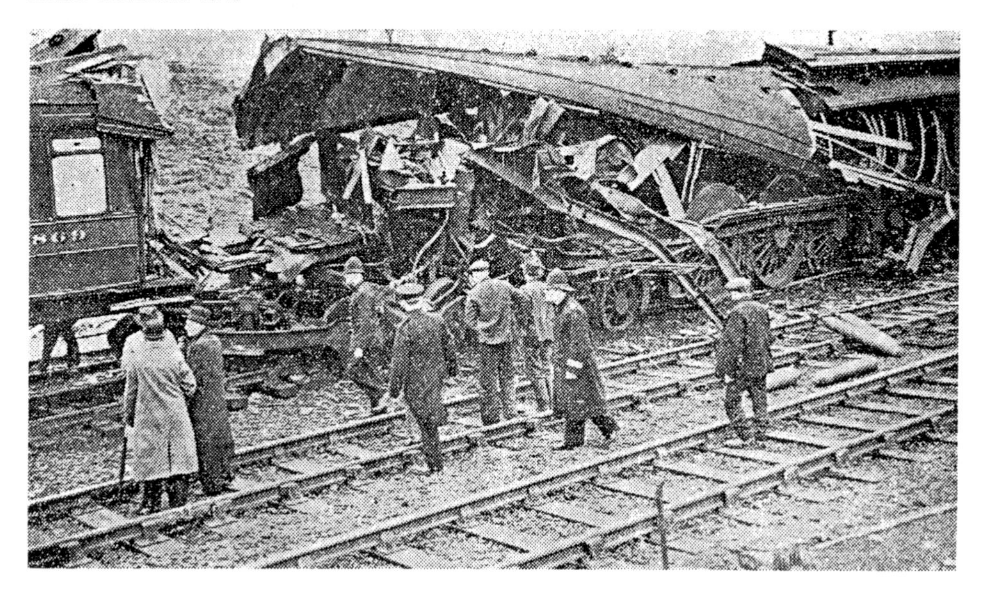

Several passengers were killed and others injured when a down train to Southend ran into the back of a Norwich-bound train which had left Liverpool Street station four minutes earlier. The engine of the Southend train smashed into the rear coach of the Norwich train, and a number of the wooden coaches were telescoped by the force of the collision. *East Anglian Daily Times*

The air raids had not ended—the Spa Pavilion at Felixstowe had received a direct hit in a raid towards the end of October—but they were generally less severe. During the whole year, it was now computed, Norwich had had 673 "alerts" lasting 1,071 hours, and 969 "crash warnings" totalling 185 hours. Twenty-one people had been killed and 104 injured. Great Yarmouth had had 767 "alerts" and 1,328 "crash warnings". Casualties had been 109 killed and 329 injured. Damage to property had been severe: 883 dwelling houses and 126 other buildings totally destroyed or damaged beyond repair, 949 houses and 197 other buildings seriously damaged, and 8,382 houses and 872 other buildings slightly damaged. Lowestoft had suffered 99 killed and 336 injured, and much of the town was badly damaged.

Life had become full of unexpected dangers. During the summer a Sudbury man had been killed when a steam-roller he was driving was hit by an aeroplane. And a Framlingham Methodist minister had died after being accidentally shot by a sentry. The normal risks were undiminished—six people died and twenty-one were injured in a train crash near Brentwood early in the year.

As is usual, adversity had brought out the best in people. During November Norwich, Cambridge and Ipswich all announced ambitious "help your neighbour" schemes. In Norwich it was the Mutual Aid Good Neighbours' Association ("MAGNA"), which sought to enrol 30,000 women. Co-operating closely with the civil defence and voluntary organisations, its aim was "to combat the misfortunes of air raids". In Cambridge the Chamber of Commerce sponsored a scheme to help traders whose premises were bombed by providing alternative premises, replacing stocks, offering clerical help and transport, and in various other ways. Ipswich operated a scheme on similar lines vigorously sponsored by the Mayor.

"Life must go on" summed up the popular attitude. Many of the familiar features of life had been maintained through all the difficulties of the year, including the normal machinery of representation of the electors. Yarmouth had secured a new Member of Parliament in Mr P.W. Jewson, who was returned unopposed in April to replace Sir Arthur Harbord, who had died. Norfolk County Council had unanimously elected Mr H.E.S. Upcher as its chairman, to succeed Alderman Russell Colman, who had resigned for health reasons after fifteen years in the job.

Even the British sense of humour seemed to have survived intact. How else can one explain the naming of a baby born in the waiting room at Peterborough North railway station Eleanour (L.N.E.R.—London and North Eastern Railway Company)?

A breakdown crane lifts one of the coaches of the London-Norwich train involved in the rail crash near Brentwood. *Eastern Daily Press*

Few people at the end of 1941 can have felt like making New Year resolutions. And yet some thought was turning towards that future, distant as it then seemed, beyond hostilities. In an editorial at the end of October, the *Eastern Daily Press* wrote:

> The Great Yarmouth Town Council has shown a commendable farsightedness in its decision to prepare an official town planning scheme for its post-war reconstruction.

Ipswich Museum must also have been thinking of posterity when in July it decided to purchase Constable's painting of Willy Lot's House on the Stour for

The bowler-hatted Secretary of State for War, Captain D. Margesson, in the Briefing Room where pilots and crews received their orders before departing on a raid; a scene during a visit to R.A.F. Wattisham in Suffolk. All ranks appear to be wearing their best uniforms. *Imperial War Museum*

£1,400 at a Sotheby's auction. And the National Trust acquired by a bequest from Lord Lothian the magnificent Jacobean mansion at Blickling, in Norfolk.

Thus was hope encouraged, in many splendid ways, at a time when the destiny of ordinary folk seemed largely out of their own hands. The war was now a global affair. Its outcome could not be settled in Europe. Nor could it be settled by the efforts or the policies of the British government and people alone.

An *Eastern Daily Press* editorial summed up the British position, as most people saw it:

> We have had heavy blows in the interval that separates this Christmas from last, but our hopes are higher today than they were then.

That was it: there was now real and well-founded hope. Britain had, with a supreme effort, mobilised her all. More powerful forces than Britain could ever hope to muster had moved in to stand side-by-side with her. Germany, and the Nazi philosophy with which it had identified itself, no longer looked all-conquering. Somewhere, still far in the future, victory seemed assured.

Notes on Sources

The principal sources for information about events and developments in East Anglia during 1941 are the various newspapers published in the region. A number of books have been published on the wartime experiences of particular towns and these have proved useful, and three manuscript accounts of air raids deposited in public libraries have also provided valuable detail. These sources have been acknowledged in the detailed references below.

This information has been supplemented by material in the Mass Observation Archive at Sussex University. Throughout the war Mass Observation regularly received reports from appointed observers, and also copies of the personal diaries of a large number of individuals. All the diary extracts quoted in this book have been drawn from this source.

For the national and international background, the standard reference works have been used: the official History of the Second World War, particularly Basil Collier's *Defence of the United Kingdom* and Richard M. Titmuss's *Problems of Social Policy*. The third volume of Sir Winston Churchill's history, *The Grand Alliance*, is another principal source.

Information about the East Anglian battalions of the Army has been obtained from the various regimental histories, but particularly from Col. W. N. Nicholson's *The Suffolk Regiment, 1928–46*.

Chapter 1

(1) Sir Winston Churchill: *The Second World War*, Volume 3, *The Grand Alliance*, p. 3.
(2) Colonel W. N. Nicholson: *The Suffolk Regiment, 1928–46.*
(3) Ibid.
(4) Captain S. W. Roskill's *The War at Sea, 1939–45* is the official history. For a full account of the Trinity House tenders at war see *Keepers of the Sea*, by Commander Richard Woodman, published by Terence Dalton, 1983.
(5) Churchill.

Chapter 2

(1) Terence H. O'Brien: *Civil Defence.*
(2) E. S. West: *Raid 'Spotting'* (unpublished MSS).
(3) Ibid.
(4) C. G. Box: *Great Yarmouth, Front Line Town, 1939–45.*
(5) B. R. Hart: *Lynn Air Raids, 1939–42* (unpublished MSS).
(6) Mass Observation Report No 884, *Ipswich Morale.*
(7) Winston Ramsey: *The Battle of Britain — Then and Now.*
(8) Paul Lund and Harry Ludlam: *Trawlers go to War.*

Chapter 3

(1) R. Douglas Brown: *East Anglia 1940.*
(2) O'Brien.
(3) Derek E. Johnson: *East Anglia at War, 1939–45.*
(4) *Cambridge Weekly News*, 20th October, 1983.
(5) Mass Observation Report No 884.
(6) Mass Observation Report No 703.

(7) Mass Observation Report No 884.
(8) *East Anglian Daily Times*, 11th January, 1972.
(9) The story of the Auxiliary Field Units is fully related in David Lampe: *The Last Ditch*, and was summarised in R. Douglas Brown: *East Anglia 1940*, pp. 94–5.
(10) Winston Ramsey: *Airfields of the Eighth — Then and Now.*
(11) Winston Ramsey: *The Battle of Britain — Then and Now.*

Chapter 4

(1) Titmuss.
(2) Mass Observation Report No 884.
(3) Nicholson.

Chapter 5

(1) A full account of the neglect of East Anglian agriculture before the war will be found in R. Douglas Brown: *East Anglia 1939.*
(2) Johnson.

Chapter 6

(1) Mass Observation Report No 703.
(2) Mass Observation Report No 884.
(3) Churchill, p. 663.

Chapter 7

(1) Churchill, p. 119.
(2) Winston Ramsey: *Airfields of the Eighth — Then and Now.*
(3) Mass Observation Report No 703.
(4) Mass Observation Report No 884.
(5) Ibid.

Chapter 8

(1) Churchill.
(2) Ramsey.
(3) Basil Collier: *A Short History of the Second World War.*
(4) O'Brien, p. 553.
(5) Sidney Harvey: *Transport Matters, No 86* (published by the Ipswich & District Historical Transport Society).

Chapter 9

(1) Nicholson. See also Tim Carew: *The Royal Norfolk Regiment.*

A Selected Bibliography

Banger, J. *Norwich at War*. Wensum Books, 1974.
Briggs, S. *Keep Smiling Through*. Weidenfeld and Nicolson, 1975.
Carew, T. *The Royal Norfolk Regiment*. Hamish Hamilton, 1967.
Churchill, W. S. *The Second World War*, vol. 3, *The Grand Alliance*. Cassell, 1950.
Collier, B. *The Defence of the United Kingdom*. H.M.S.O., 1957.
Collier, B. *A Short History of the Second World War*. Collins, 1967.
Jenkins, F. *Lowestoft — Port War, 1939–45*. W. S. Cowell, Ipswich, n.d.; Panda Books, Lowestoft, 1984.
Johnson, D. E. *East Anglia at War, 1939–45*. Jarrold, 1978.
Lampe, D. *The Last Ditch*. Cassell, 1968.
Lund, P. and Ludlam, H. *Trawlers go to War*. New English Library, 1972.
Malster, R. *Saved from the Sea*. Terence Dalton, 1974.
Moir, G. *The Suffolk Regiment*. Leo Cooper, 1969.
Nicholson, W. N. *The Suffolk Regiment, 1928–46*. East Anglian Magazine, n.d.
O'Brien, T. H. *Civil Defence*. H.M.S.O., 1955.
Ramsey, W. *Airfields of the Eighth — Then and Now*. Battle of Britain Prints International, 1978.
Roskill, S. W. *The War at Sea, 1939–45*. H.M.S.O., 1954.
Titmuss, R. M. *Problems of Social Policy*. H.M.S.O., 1950.
Bury Free Press
Cambridge Daily News
East Anglian Daily Times
Eastern Daily Press
Lynn Advertiser
Norfolk and Norwich Weekly Press

Index